GOLD COAST
ALCHEMY

By Tracey Broussard

GOLD COAST ALCHEMY

Craft and Concept Cocktails
from Miami to the Palm Beaches

By Tracey Broussard

Published by LCIX Editions
Mt. Pleasant, SC
www.lcixllc.com

For Laura, Max, Sam and Kenton.
A mother couldn't ask for a better krewe.

And for my grandchildren, Remy, Rory and Little Laura.
You put the happy in my happy hours.

TABLE OF CONTENTS

Introduction 10

Elevate the Experience 16

MIAMI. 19

    Aviation 22

    La Pina Loca from R House, Wynwood 24

    A5 Fat-Washed Old Fashioned 26

    Messi Effect 28

    Launch Point. 30

HALLANDALE. 33

    The Accountant's Margarita 34

    Sing Like a Canary 36

    The Derby Daiquiri. 38

    Florida Man Mule 40

    DiMaggio Affogato. 42

HOLLYWOOD 45

    Body Heat 46

    Jimmy Blue Eyes 48

    Beach Water. 50

    Maraja's Paradise. 52

    It's No Big Dill. 54

DANIA BEACH. 57

Chula 58

Rumrunner 60

Fender Bender 62

Monkey Gland 64

Orange Blossom Crunch. 66

FORT LAUDERDALE 69

The Rat Takes the Cup 70

Spicy Avocado Margarita. 72

Florida Old Fashioned. 74

Anthony's Paper Plane 76

Stacey's Favorite Punch. 78

POMPANO BEACH 81

Passion Fruit Batida. 82

Ship Sank Sangria 84

Sorel Sparkler 86

Perfect Storm. 88

Coquito 90

BOCA RATON 93

What a Wonderful World Caipirinha .96

Arnold Palmer Smash 98

Ai Papi Double. 100

Florida Heat 102

Wake the Dead. 104

DELRAY BEACH **107**

 Orange Grove House of Refuge 108

 Barefoot Mailman 110

 Boozy Strawberry Shake 112

 Train Wrecked 114

 Pineapple Paradise 116

BOYNTON BEACH **119**

 Ladybug Landing 120

 GiGi Refresher 122

 Flying Chancleta 124

 Mango Cosmo 126

 Coconut Coquimbo 128

PALM BEACH **131**

 Caramel Popcorn Old Fashioned 134

 Jimmy Red Sour 136

 Lucky in Love Lycheetini 138

 Lilly Paloma 140

 The Last Train to Paradise 142

Gold Coast Bar Stock 144

Accessories 145

Acknowledgements 149

About the Author 152

ORANGE GROVE HOUSE OF REFUGE NO. 3
1876 - 1927

One of several built by Treasury Department between Cape Canaveral and Cape Florida for rescue and sustenance of shipwrecked. Named for wild sour orange grove nearby. H. D. Pierce, first keeper, arrived with family May 1876. Here August 15, 1876, was born the first white girl between Jupiter and Miami -- (Mrs.) Lillie Pierce Voss. Stephen N. Andrews was last keeper, from September 1877 to October 1, 1896. Area's first post office, Zion, was located in House from 1888 to 1892. Mrs. Annie E. Andrews postmaster. House burned March 2, 1927.

JONATHAN DICKINSON CHAPTER,
NATIONAL SOCIETY, DAUGHTERS OF THE AMERICAN REVOLUTION
IN COOPERATION WITH
THE FLORIDA HISTORICAL SOCIETY
FLORIDA BOARD OF PARKS AND HISTORIC MEMORIALS

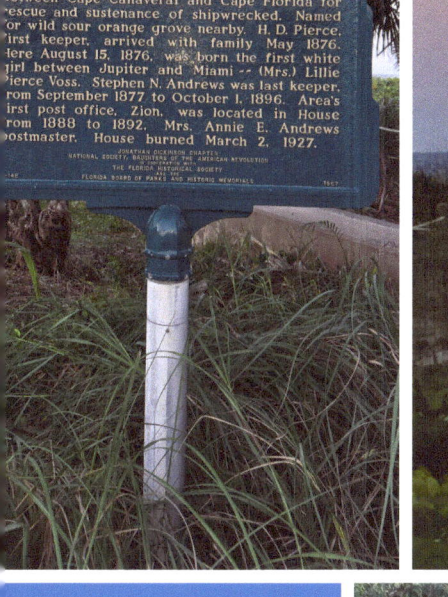

GOLD DUST MOTEL

RESCUE

MRP

INTRODUCTION

Florida's Gold Coast is hot. It is sultry, sweltering, sexy. Cooling winds and swirling hurricanes blow in from the Atlantic Ocean. Humidity hovers everywhere, reducing the body's ability to cool itself. Here you feel hotter because your core temperature actually is hotter.

Those of us who love and live in the Gold Coast embrace the heat. Our senses are stirred by bright and bold flavors and colors, our nights illuminated by neon and temptation. We dive into the ocean of our cities' offerings the same way we would into a wave: with joy and childlike exuberance.

We welcome you to join us.

Put on your sunscreen, pull up a beach chair, and stick your toes in the sand. Pour some chilled Jupina into your pink Stanley cup and top it with coconut rum for a high-low highball. Sip as you build a sand castle. Meditate on the ephemeral nature of existence as the water dissolves your creation.

We might not get tomorrow, but we have today.

Make the most of it with a café con leche or a Cafecito after the beach. Stop off at El Palacio De Los Jugos for a Cubano sandwich and a fresh pressed guava juice — just like Abuelita used to make.

After the sun sets, don your Dior, jump into your Maserati and valet at the Dirty French Steakhouse. Yeah. We're flashy. And we're not sorry about it. Before dinner sip on a Gold Dollar – reposado tequila, passionfruit, pineapple and champagne. Money never tasted so good.

Money, you may think, is why our area is referred to as the Gold Coast. It's hard to think of Florida's blue waters without imagining the pirate ships and Spanish galleons of yore.

There are over 5,000 shipwrecks off of the coast of Florida, many of which are still unexplored. Their treasures are waiting to be plundered, just as pirates Sir Frances Drake, Calico Jack and Anne Bonny did along our shores.

Calico Jack, in fact, married Anne Bonny, a female pirate. He welcomed other female pirates to join his merry crew.

It is fitting that female pirates roamed the waters beside the only major American city founded by a woman.

Julia Tuttle owned the property upon which Miami was built. Her vision, along with her 640 acres, slowly transformed wilderness into the city we know and love today.

Continue up the coast of Miami to Palm Beach and you will experience the beauty and bounty of our Gold Coast.

Before Henry Flagler brought his railroad to the towns — changing history and the landscape forever — our cities were founded mostly by farmers. Everything from pineapples to tomatoes to corn thrived, attracting a melting pot of people from all corners of the world.

This alone would be reason to call ourselves the Gold Coast. But neither pirates nor produce are responsible for that moniker. The value of the area's real estate, along with the ritzy lifestyles of our population caused the term to be coined in the early 1980's.

Since the 80's we have seen South Beach turn from a retirees' oasis into a hotspot for models and moguls. Palm Beach is home to a president while Boca Raton, Fort Lauderdale, Key Biscayne, and Coral Gables house a bounty of billionaires.

It is perhaps the wacky and wanton ways of our wealthiest that has given rise to Florida Man. If you aren't familiar with Florida Man, please put this book down and Google it. Try not to laugh.

The Florida Man phenomenon is far from the first time our brethren have made the news.

Though the Gold Coast was founded and then populated by talented, hard-working, adventurous pioneers, we have had more than our share of shady characters. And though we may not be the Bourbon Trail, we have a shady distillery. Located in Fort Lauderdale, Shady Distillery celebrates the offbeat characters lurking in our history and around our corners.

We also have distilleries named for one of our most beloved writers, Ernest Hemingway. Named after his boat Pilar, Papa's Pilar celebrates all that is Hemingway along with making a superior rum.

We have a Wicked Dolphin distillery, as well as Revenge Rum. Born from a 21-year-old's first sip of a daiquiri, founder, Chris Bolt, has kept the spirit of our founders alive by housing his business in a historic firehouse.

Steel Tie Spirits Co. in West Palm Beach is a family operation named for the ancestor who wouldn't stop offering cocktails to his fellow railroad workers. His boss declared that the only way to keep the man working was to put a steel tie on him.

The stories we tell on the Gold Coast are as sweet and spectacular as our cocktails and lifestyles.

Although sweet drinks may not be de rigueur in popular mixology today, their home is entrenched here in South Florida. There's a reason why many of us reach for sugary drinks in the heat. The body uses glucose for energy. Sugar also gives our brains a hit of dopamine, the feel-good hormone that keeps us craving more.

We also like fruit here. A lot. We grow it, we freeze it, we cook with it, we add it to our drinks and we give our excess to our friends. If you haven't tried lychees, loquats, mango, papaya, mamey, guava, passionfruit or dragon fruit, you're missing out. Swap out some of these for the fruits in your favorite recipes. You won't be sorry.

Speaking of swapping out, almost every recipe here can be altered. We have included Gold Coast distilleries and Florida ingredients whenever possible. Craft cocktails can be defined as a cocktail that's made with quality ingredients and a high level of skill or technique in its execution.

Concept cocktails, on the other hand, are a personal expression of an idea in cocktail form.

Here we will share primarily concept cocktails, based on histories, stories and traditions that make up Florida's Gold Coast. Create the recipes as written or make them your own. Not all of the ingredients listed may be available in your area, but chances are good that you can find something similar wherever you are. Don't be afraid to experiment and enjoy the process.

A look at the map of South Florida will show that there are many cities and neighborhoods that are not named in our text. For simplicity's sake, we divided the chapters into 10 cities that are along the actual coast of South Florida. There are times we will point out places that are a short drive west. The Gold Coast is not just pretty beaches. We have botanical gardens, nature preserves, hiking trails, mangrove swamps and a river of grass — the Everglades.

Come raise a glass with us. Our riches are vast, plentiful and here for the sharing.

Cheers.

ELEVATE THE EXPERIENCE

There are many facets of the word "craft" that bring to mind a manner in which something can be elevated. Planning and executing are components as are skill levels and the materials used. The higher the qualities of all of the above, the better chances we have to approach a creation that is not merely art but something sublime.

What constitutes art and what stands out as sublime are subjective. Not unlike Wikipedia's definition of craft, both can be traced back to the "structures, values, history and identities of the communities in which they are located."

A great cocktail, like a great bite of food, is the result of layering.

It can be as complex as the A5 Fat-Washed Old Fashioned in our Miami chapter, relying on components such as rendered fat from a superb steak, specific spirits and a smoking gun finish.

Or it can be far simpler. Swapping out Pink Ting grapefruit soda for grapefruit juice in our Lilly Paloma. Serving it in a pink-hued flamingo shaped glass, preferably while wearing a Lilly Pulitzer dress sans underwear.

One could argue that the former is a craft cocktail while the latter is a concept cocktail. Potato potah-to.

Both evoke a sense of time and place. Each is visually stunning and tastes fantastic. It has been argued that both craft and concept cocktails could be considered pretentious or silly. No matter.

How you compose your cocktails, your meals, your reading list, or your daily activities can be elevated with one question. Does it bring you joy? Will it make you smile? Can adding an ingredient, a special serving dish or glass, a local, seasonal herb or fruit make what you're creating look or taste better? Will it surprise or delight?

Is it fun? Will it convey love and care to the people in your life that you're preparing it for?

There are no rules here. Intention is what matters. Play around. Experiment. Maybe invest in some new bar tools and fun gadgets such as a smoking gun or Flavourblaster. Or, you could clean out your pantry. Check for items that will expire soon and experiment. Write down the successful ones so that you won't forget what you did.

The efforts you put into elevating your experiences lead to fond memories. Throughout the book we will occasionally offer suggestions with which to elevate our cocktail recipes. Give them a try or do your own thing. Snap a pic and write to us with your results. Sharing is caring. Tag me on Instagram @tracey.broussard so I can pass along the fun.

MIAMI

Miami was incorporated in 1896 and just a month later began calling itself the Magic City.

It rose quickly after Julia Tuttle, the "Mother of Miami," moved to town in 1891. Seeing Miami's potential, she bought land and encouraged others to invest and develop. Her persistence was such that she sent Henry Flagler a bouquet of flowers after a freeze destroyed orange groves in central Florida. She realized that the extension of his railroad would help her realize the big dreams she had for the city.

Flagler complied and laid out the town in 1895. When Miami was incorporated in 1896, the residents wanted to honor him by naming the town "Flagler." He declined, persuading them to keep the Indian name: Miami.

Paleo-Indians discovered Miami over 10,000 years ago. After that the Tequesta people, a Native American tribe, thrived for almost 2,000 years. Though the Miccosukee and Seminoles arrived in the 1700's, Miami was actually named for the Native American tribe that lived around Lake Okeechobee from 500 BC to the 17th or 18th century. Mayaimi, the name of the tribe, is also the historic name of Lake Okeechobee, meaning "big water."

The Atlantic Ocean, Key Biscayne and Lake Okeechobe are just some of the bodies of water that make up Miami's landscape. The Cruise Capital of the World is another of the Magic City's monikers, as is the Gateway to the Americas, due to its positioning as a crossroad between North and South America.

More cheeky nicknames include The 305, Miami's original area code; The Capital of South America, referring to our large Latin American population; The Sixth Borough, a nod to the New Yorkers who have relocated to Miami; and what might be my personal favorite, A Sunny Place for Shady People.

The neighborhoods that make up Miami are as unique and vibrant as the people who inhabit them. While we love our beaches, it would be a mistake to dismiss the history, culture, cuisines and unique architecture of neighborhoods such as Coconut Grove, MiMo, Little Havana, Little Haiti, Wynwood, the Miami Design District and more.

Check out www.miamiandbeaches.com, Lonely Planet, and Time Out Miami for comprehensive overviews of our area's many offerings.

AVIATION

Eva Mendes welcomes you to Miami with a sultry "Bienvenido a Miami!" from the driver's seat of her hot white convertible.

Will Smith deplanes from a private jet onto the red carpet so graciously prepared for him in his iconic "Miami" video.

Your arrival in Miami might not be as glamorous. Cheer up: we welcome you to Miami with an Aviation, your just reward for having survived Miami International Airport. Yeah, we know, we know, we're working on it; MIA's Modernization in Action consists of nearly $9 billion in maintenance upgrades and improvements over the next 10 years.

The Aviation, on the other hand, needs no improvement. It was invented by Hugo Ensslin, head bartender at New York City's Hotel Wallick, in the early part of the 20th century. A pre-Prohibition cocktail that's a variation of the gin sour, the cocktail's sweet notes come from the addition of maraschino liqueur and include floral notes from crème de violette. Our version uses Meyer lemons, which thrive in Miami's subtropical climate. Their taste is less acidic than regular lemons with a floral scent that includes notes of bergamot.

Ingredients

2 ounces gin
½ ounce maraschino liqueur
¾ ounce freshly squeezed Meyer lemon juice
¼ ounce crème de violette

Directions

Combine all ingredients in an ice-filled shaker. Shake vigorously for 30 seconds and double-strain into a chilled cocktail glass. Garnish with sour cherry, brandied cherry or Filthy Amarena Cherry.

Elevate

Elevate your Aviation by garnishing with an Amarena cherry made by Miami's own Filthy foods. These wild Italian Amarena cherries are sourced in Northern Italy and slow-cooked at the Filthy factory in Miami in copper pots. They deliver a rich and complex flavor with a sweet front and tart finish.

LA PINA LOCA

Just north of Miami, the walls of Wynwood are bejeweled with the works of some of the world's most talented street artists. This Wynwood arts district is home to funky art galleries, warehouses converted to craft breweries, a graffiti museum and the stomping ground of all manner of families, hipsters, artists, and queens. While you may not bump into Starina, the drag queen from the iconic Robin Williams and Nathan Lane movie *The Birdcage*, you will find a talented cast of queens at R House's drag brunch. You will also find a showstopping take on a piña colada, the La Piña Loca. Served in a hollowed-out pineapple with sparklers and five shots, the La Piña Loca is the perfect party libation. Loca, in Spanish, means madwoman or queen. In our opinion, La Piña Loca is a little bit of both.

Ingredients

3 ounces light rum
3 ounces coconut rum
3 ounces pineapple juice
3 ounces organic cream of coconut
¾ ounce fresh lime juice
Ice

Garnish:

One whole pineapple
Flamingo straws
Tiki umbrellas
Dehydrated citrus
2 sparklers

Directions

Remove the pulp of the whole pineapple and reserve it to make the fresh pineapple juice.

Make pineapple juice by putting pineapple cubes through a juicer or pulsing in a high-speed blender. Strain through a fine mesh strainer, if desired.

To make the piña colada, add all ingredients to a blender and pulse until combined. Pour into the hollowed-out pineapple and add garnishes and sparklers. Serve on a bamboo tray lined with 5 shots of rum.

A5 FAT-WASHED OLD FASHIONED

Who better to take the Old Fashioned to new heights than Michelin-starred chef Michael Mina? At Mina's luxe Bourbon Steak Miami, the Old Fashioned is prepared by fat-washing Jefferson's Reserve Bourbon utilizing the trimmings of Mina's A5 New York strip. A5 is the highest grade for the highest quality of Japanese Wagyu steak. The rating is based on a 1-12 scale with one being the lowest and 12 being the highest, on the BMS — Beef Marbling Standard. Unlike the tears many of us shed due to a high BMI score, a steak with a high BMS brings tears of joy. It follows suit that a cocktail prepared with perfectly seasoned A5 tallow will be tasty, complex and marbled with flavor. After mixing, the drink is chilled in a Yarai * and then finished under a smoke-filled dome.

Ingredients

2 ounces tallow-washed Jefferson's Reserve Bourbon
¼ ounce simple syrup
3 dashes of orange bitters
3 dashes of Angostura bitters

Directions

Combine all the ingredients in a Yarai *. Add ice. Stir for 10 seconds. Stir into a double rock glass and stamp ice. Smoke in a glass dome.

For the tallow-washed bourbon: Start by rendering the trimmings of Michael Mina's A5 New York strip. Clean the tallow and refrigerate until solid. Add 2 tablespoons for every 750 ml of Bourbon. Let it rest overnight then refrigerate until the tallow has solidified. Remove tallow solids and strain.

*A Yarai is a heavy mixing glass named for the Japanese diamond pattern etched on the outside. There are glass and stainless-steel versions with narrow spouts for ease and smoothness when pouring.

Elevate

There are an abundance of cocktail smokers and glass domes available online, should you wish to add to your bartending arsenal. Here is a list of the top 7 for 2024 as reviewed by foodandwine.com:

The 7 Best Cocktail Smokers of 2024, Tested & Reviewed (foodandwine. com)

Tasting Notes

Jefferson's Reserve Bourbon is a small batch blend of mature bourbons that's the oldest and most robust bourbon in the Jefferson's family. Honey and nutmeg are detectable on the nose, with notes of caramel, toffee and cinnamon flavor on the tongue. It has a medium-long and dry finish with a little spiciness on the palate.

MESSI EFFECT

Good things come when Lionel Messi moves to Miami. Almost overnight the value of the Inter Miami soccer team skyrocketed to $1.5 billion. It's estimated that Messi's presence alone may increase Miami tourism up to 10%, resulting in tourist expenditures of around $400 million. That is cause to cheer.

Add that to Messi's humility and charitable endeavors, and it's reason enough to honor him with his own cocktail. Besides establishing the Leo Messi Foundation, which helps provide needy children with medical care, education and the opportunity to participate in sports, he has made significant donations to a legion of charities including UNICEF, cancer research and much more.

To be worthy of the Messi name, a drink in his honor should contain his favorite beverage — mate, pronounced "maa tay." Made from the leaves of the yerba mate plant, mate is an integral part of Argentinian life. So much so that it even has its own drinking vessel: a gourd (called mate as well) and a Latin American tea straw called a bombilla.

You won't need a gourd or bombilla for this cocktail, but it does call for a mate simple syrup and pisco — a white brandy made in Peru from muscat grapes. Pisco's herbal and earthy flavors complement the bold taste of mate.

Ingredients

2 ounces pisco
1 ounce freshly squeezed lime juice
½ ounce yerba mate simple syrup

1 egg white
Angostura bitters or Fernet Branca

Directions

Add pisco, lime juice, simple syrup and egg white into a shaker and dry shake. Pour into a blender with three ice cubes. Blend until frothy. Pour into a Nick & Nora or rocks glass. Garnish with a few drops of Angostura bitters or a few drops of Fernet Branca. Use a toothpick to swirl the bitters into a design, if you wish.

LAUNCH POINT

The Bill Baggs Cape Florida State Park on Key Biscayne is home to the Cape Florida Lighthouse. Not only is its beach frequently ranked as one of the top 10 nationwide, but it also represents a beacon for freedom.

The lighthouse stands on the site of one of the major launch points of the Underground Saltwater Railroad. This was a coastal escape route between 1821 and 1861. Here, fugitives would launch dugout canoes or small boats, as well as pay for passage on Bahamian vessels to find freedom in the British-controlled Bahamas. Says historian Nadege Green, "It is a sight where Black people stole themselves back, repossessed themselves from the horror of slavery."

In honor of those brave people who journeyed through the muck and marshes of undeveloped Florida to face pirates and storms en route to the Bahamas and the promise of freedom, we offer you a cocktail with a trace of salt.

Ingredients

½ ounce Manzanilla sherry
¼ ounce Hendrick's gin
¼ ounce elderflower liqueur
3 ounces Brut Champagne or sparkling wine
2 drops lemon bitters

Directions

Add sherry, gin and elderflower liqueur into an ice-filled shaker. Shake vigorously. Strain into a coupe glass. Top with sparkling wine. Add bitters. Give a gentle stir. Garnish with a lemon twist.

Tasting Notes

A 1997 Harvard study showed that salt enhances flavor by suppressing bitterness. It also enhances the taste of fresh flavors — think salted watermelon or cantaloupe. Salt can be added to the rim of a cocktail glass, such as in a margarita, or added to the ingredients in a saline form by mixing salt and water. Some mixologists microdose all their cocktails with saline, while others play with salty additions such as soy or Worchester sauce.

Another option is to use ingredients that have an inherent saltiness such as Manzanilla Sherry. Aged in the seaside city of Barrameda, Spain, Manzanilla Sherry is known for its salty taste and coastal aroma.

Progress. Innovation. Opportunity.

HALLANDALE

Hallandale began as a sleepy agricultural town settled by Swedish farmers. Though the entirety of the Gold Coast was prime territory for bootleggers and rumrunners, it wasn't until Prohibition ended that Hallandale became a hotbed of sin.

The notorious Jewish gangster Meyer Lansky, also known as The Mob's Accountant, saw potential when he turned a former tomato packing shed into a casino. Before long, Hallandale was a gambler's paradise. The local farmers profited by selling their produce to the casinos, which also provided many jobs to locals.

Legal slot machines could be found from drug stores to fishing camps and the boulevard was lined with casinos and drinking establishments. Banks flocked to the city to handle the money, resulting in the city's moniker, "The Wall Street of the South."

Horse and dog racing were also popular entertainment and gambling venues in Hallandale, with Gulfstream Park still operating today as a racetrack, shopping and dining mecca.

Sometimes referred to as "Canada's southernmost city," Hallandale is also a popular destination for snowbirds from Quebec, Canada.

For weekly listings of local activities and special events, check out www.floridasuntimes.com.

THE ACCOUNTANT'S MARGARITA

Wise guys and the Gold Coast go together like peas and carrots. Gambling in Broward County generated so much money that the mafia had an understanding — no killings in Broward.

This was good for Meyer Lansky, casino entrepreneur and the mob's accountant. Not only was Lansky not murdered, but in his entire career only served 24 days in jail. Though his prison time included delivered meals it's doubtful that he had access to margaritas.

Not to be confused with Lansky, Meyer lemons were introduced to the U.S. by Frank Meyer. Frank came across the fruit while visiting Peking, China in 1908. A hybrid of a mandarin and a lemon, Meyer lemons are sweeter than other lemons. The trees symbolize longevity and prosperity. The skin also smells like heaven, with sweet, floral notes and is edible.

Meyer lemon trees flourish on the Gold Coast. They are a great addition anywhere that you would normally find lemon.

Ingredients

2 tablespoons Meyer lemon juice
2 tablespoons lime juice
2 tablespoons Patron Silver
1 tablespoon sweetener
1 teaspoon triple sec

Sweet and Salty Citrus Rim

¼ cup kosher salt
1/8 cup sugar
Zest of one Meyer lemon
Zest of ½ lime

Directions

Rim a chilled margarita glass with the sweet and salty mixture. Set aside. Combine margarita ingredients in an ice-filled shaker. Strain into the rimmed margarita glass.

SING LIKE A CANARY

Philip "The Stick" Kovolick was found sealed in a steel drum at the bottom of a rock pit in Hallandale. So much for that "No killings in Broward" rule. A close associate of Meyer Lansky, Kovolick had been indicted in New York, charged with "consorting with known criminals for unlawful purposes."

Was someone afraid that The Stick would sing like a canary if put on trial? We'll probably never know.

What we do know is that the Sing Like a Canary cocktail tastes as pretty as it looks. It's the perfect pick-me-up for the rainy afternoon doldrums.

The fifth rainiest state, Florida is also the lightning capital of the U.S. Afternoon thunderstorms are so common that those of us in the know plan our days around them.

Relax. Have a drink. The storm will be over before you know it.

Ingredients

1 ounce pineapple rum
3 ounces prosecco
½ ounce guava juice

Directions

Add pineapple rum and guava juice to a chilled Champagne flute. Top with prosecco. Give a gentle stir with a bar spoon. Serve in a birdcage hanging from a tree branch.

THE DERBY DAIQUIRI

The Derby Daiquiri is one of those drinks that is greater than the sum of its parts. Though the ingredients are few — rum, orange juice, lime juice, simple syrup — together they create a fitting tribute to the Florida Derby.

Held in late March of every year, the Florida Derby is a Triple Crown Primer raced at Gulfstream Park.

In 1959, the Florida Derby held a contest to find a signature cocktail. The winning drink was the Derby Daiquiri, created by Mariano Licudine. Licudine was a bartender at Fort Lauderdale's famous Mai-Kai restaurant.

The Mai-Kai had a long and storied history with Puerto Rican rum, making it a natural for this cocktail. The match led to not only a pre-Florida Derby race called the Mai-Kai Rum Cup (wherein the winning jockey received a sterling silver "Derby Cup" and a 5-gallon wooden barrel filled with Puerto Rican rum), but other tales of mischief and mobile tiki huts from which Licundine would serve his winning drink to travelers.

An excellent article about the daiquiri and its history can be found here: The Derby Daiquiri: The Mai-Kai's '$100,000 drink' is worth its weight in gold - The Atomic Grog (slammie.com)

Ingredients

1 ounce orange juice
½ ounce lime juice
½ ounce simple syrup
1 ½ ounces light Puerto Rican rum

Directions

Combine all ingredients in a blender with one cup crushed ice. Blend until it is a smooth, liquid consistency. Serve in a chilled daiquiri glass.

FLORIDA MAN MULE

"Florida man breaks into rabbi's house, drinks his vodka and sleeps in his bed."

Have you heard of Florida Man? Wikipedia defines Florida Man as "an alleged prevalence of people performing irrational or maniacal actions in the U.S. state of Florida."

Though Florida Man is responsible for many statewide shenanigans — such as throwing an alligator through a Wendy's drive-thru window — the above-mentioned Goldilocks incident took place in Hallandale.

Had our Florida Man realized that the third most common tree in Hallandale is the mango, he might have mixed the rabbi's vodka in a blender with some frozen chunks, ginger beer and lime juice for a riff on a mule.

Mules are comprised of vodka, ginger beer and lime. They are traditionally served in a copper cup. Be sure to use a cup lined with stainless steel to avoid copper leaching into your drink. Alternatively, mix up a big batch of mango mules for parties. Pour from a pretty glass pitcher into frosted wine glasses.

In not-so-maniacal news, a Florida man took a bus to Kentucky and then rode a mule 1,500 miles to Wyoming. All for the sake of keeping his word to his granddaughter. And you thought all of the stories from Florida were strange.

Ingredients

3 ounces vodka
½ cup frozen mango
3 tablespoons lime juice
1 tablespoon simple syrup
¾ cup ginger beer

Directions

Place everything except the ginger beer into a blender. Blend until frothy. Pour into a chilled glass and garnish with a mango slice and/or lime wheel.

DIMAGGIO AFFOGATO

Follow in Joe DiMaggio's footsteps at the Northern tip of Hallandale. Maintained by the city of Hollywood, the Joe DiMaggio park is home to a 24-acre park that is dog-friendly, kid-friendly and a favorite place for the Yankee Clipper to take a stroll during his sunset years.

A resident of Hallandale's Harbor Island, DiMaggio moved to Florida in 1985. A shy and gracious man, Joe was frequently approached by gobsmacked fans while dining out or meeting up with friends around town. He gladly signed autographs and posed for pictures, stating that it was the price you paid for being famous.

In later years, DiMaggio lent his name to the pediatric wing of Hollywood's Memorial Hospital, the motto of which is, "Whether rich or poor, no child is turned away."

If leading the Yankees in nine World Series championships wasn't enough, DiMaggio also helped to usher in a new age of coffee drinking in America. The face behind Mr. Coffee for 14 years, Joe was known to enjoy as many as 12 cups in a day.

Ingredients

1 ½ ounces espresso liqueur
½ ounce crème de cacao
1 ounce freshly brewed, hot Cuban coffee
1 scoop vanilla ice cream or gelato

Directions

Combine all ingredients in a blender with 4 ice cubes. Blend until frothy. Pour into a chilled coupe glass. Garnish with a sprinkling of cocoa powder and coffee beans.

Switch it Up

Traditionally affogato is eaten as dessert and served as a scoop of gelato with espresso poured over it. Feel free to omit the blender and ice cubes if you'd rather spoon than sip your affogato. Switch out the vanilla ice cream for chocolate or add some crumbled biscotti for texture. Toasted hazelnuts make a nice garnish as well.

Diamond of the Gold Coast

HOLLYWOOD

Joseph W. Young founded Hollywood, Florida in the 1920's. He named it after the Hollywood located in Southern California, and set out to establish his dream town.

Young spent millions creating roads and infrastructure and enticing investors to build in his city. Besides hoping to create a home for the film industry in the south, he wanted this city to be, "a city for everyone — from the opulent at the top of the industrial and social ladder to the most humble of working people."

He succeeded. Hollywood is now considered the most diverse city in Florida.

The popular Hollywood Beach Broadwalk is a 2.5-mile promenade along the Atlantic Ocean. There you can bike ride, rollerblade, take a leisurely stroll, or enjoy a meal at one of the many seaside cafes. The outdoor Hollywood Beach Theater features free concerts, and the kids can have a blast splashing in the water playground at Charnow Park.

Check out the city's website at www.hollywoodfl.org for fun and usually free family activities. A recent search turned up outdoor movie nights at the Young Circle Arts Park, cardboard boat races at the City of Hollywood Marina and a concert of Beatles music at TY Park.

BODY HEAT

Body Heat is a thriller filmed in 1981 starring Kathleen Turner and William Hurt. Turner plays a femme fatale who seduces Hurt into killing her husband so she can inherit his money. Pivotal scenes were filmed at the bandshell on the Hollywood broadwalk and in Nick's Bar — a Hollywood Beach institution since 1980.While there is clearly body heat in the film, it is set during a literal heatwave.

Soon after our lovers first meet, Hurt buys Turner a snow cone on the broadwalk, which she spills down the front of her shirt. Turner gazes at Hurt, "You don't want to lick it off?" She's turned up the heat and it's game on.

Like a snow cone, this drink is slushy. Unlike most frozen drinks, however, it's not sweet. This Body Heat is banana forward, thanks to equal parts banana liqueur to coconut rum. The original recipe calls for pineapple juice and regular lemon juice. We use fresh pineapple and Meyer lemon juice here.

Ingredients

1 ounce Wicked Dolphin coconut rum
1 ounce banana liqueur
1 spear chopped fresh pineapple
½ ounce Meyer lemon juice
2 dashes grenadine
1 cup crushed ice

Directions

Add all ingredients except grenadine into a blender and pulse. Pour into a chilled highball glass. Add grenadine.

JIMMY BLUE EYES

Not long after I moved into my first Florida home, I padded to the sidewalk to collect the morning paper. My neighbor stood a few steps away, reading the headline and shaking his head. "Organized crime? Washington is organized crime," he said.

That neighbor was Jimmy Alo, aka "Jimmy Blue Eyes," a high-ranking capo in the Genovese crime family and Meyer Lansky's partner.

I have no idea what crimes Jimmy did or did not commit. What I do know is that he was charming, dapper and an interesting neighbor. One never knew when he would be in the mood to share some history of crimes against Italians in the United States, or mob-related tidbits.

"Bugsy Seigal?" He said to me one day. "We always got blamed for it but we didn't kill him. He used to beat his girlfriend. It was her brother that killed Bugsy."

"Did you ever kill anyone?" I asked him.

"No," he answered. "But if anyone did get killed it was just business."

Ingredients

1 ounce blue curacao
2 ounces vodka
½ ounce J.F. Haden's Lychee Liqueur
1 ounce lime

Directions

Add all ingredients into an ice-filled shaker. Strain into an ice-filled Collins glass. Garnish with a lemon twist.

BEACH WATER

Texans can keep their ranch water (not that we have anything against it, mind you). Here we sip Beach Water.

Beach Water is our easiest cocktail. You can use Jupina, a pineapple-flavored soda that made its way from Cuba to a factory in Hialeah to the entirety of South Florida's beaches. Or you can use a bottle of Jarritos. Made with natural fruit, Jarritos comes in flavors like guava, mandarin, lime, watermelon and more.

The sun and sand are hot and the ocean may be warm but the Jarritos and Jupinas are icy cold. Dip your hand into the ice-filled cooler and fish one out. Sip a few sweet ounces and then add an ounce or so of vodka and a squeeze of lime.

Salud.

Ingredients

1 bottle chilled Jupina
1 ounce vodka
Squeeze of lime

Directions

Drink a couple of sips of Jupina. Add vodka and lime.

MARAJA'S PARADISE

Some people are beach bums. Others feel more at home under trees or canoeing the wetlands. We are blessed with both in South Florida.

Drive west on Hollywood Boulevard and it turns into Pines Boulevard and the city of Pembroke Pines. Here you will find 28 parks, among which is the Chapel Trail Park Nature Preserve.

Home to 120 species of birds, deer, marsh rabbits, alligators and more, the park is 450 acres with a 1,650 foot-long boardwalk, canoe rentals and free admission.

Named "All-America City," Pembroke Pines is known for its cultural diversity, commitment to the arts (Check out The Frank, a free two-story art gallery in the Pembroke Pines City Center), affordable golf and world-class shopping.

Here, we encourage you to pick your own paradise.

The Maraja's Paradise was created my mixologist Maraja at Baoshi Food Hall, a popular Asian food hall and bar in Pembroke Pines.

Ingredients

2 ounces Stella Rosa Tropical Passion Brandy
1 ounce Peach Schnapps
1 ounces strawberry puree
1 ounce pineapple juice

Directions

Combine all ingredients except pineapple juice in a cocktail shaker. Shake and strain into a tall, ice-filled, chilled glass. Top with pineapple juice. Garnish with fresh fruit.

IT'S NO BIG DILL

Dill thrives in South Florida from September through December. Though it may not be the first herb you think of when considering cocktail ingredients, it's a surprisingly tasty one. Part of the same vegetable family as celery, dill pairs especially well with vodka-based drinks. Dill also complements cucumbers, as we all know and love when we crunch a dill pickle.

Created by mixologist Rob Husted, It's No Big Dill is a fun drink. It makes sense when you consider that Rob's passion is to travel the world to help bartenders make better cocktails and have more fun behind the bar. You can catch Rob flipping bottles in the Alan Jackson video, "It's 5 O'Clock Somewhere," and, if you're lucky, in person at Steel Tie Distillery in Palm Beach.

Ingredients

2 ounces Steel Tie Spirits Vodka
8 drops saline solution
1 ounce Claussen pickle juice
¾ ounce simple syrup
1 dash cucumber bitters
1 dash smoked bitters

Directions

Combine all ingredients in a mixing glass filled all of the way with ice. Stir and strain into a chilled coupe glass. Garnish with a fresh dill sprig. Plate with two pickle spears topped with seasoning (Rob uses Steel Tie Spirits wicked seasoning house blend) on a wooden board. You can use a spicy blend such as Tajin, or whatever your favorite savory seasoning might be. Place cocktail on the board for serving.

Saline Solution

¼ ounce Kosher salt
2 ounces room temperature water

Directions

Combine ingredients in a shaker with no ice. Shake hard for a minute and strain into an eye dropper.

DANIA BEACH

The first city in Broward County, Dania Beach was developed in the 1880's and settled by 12 Danish families from Chicago. Three years after the first group, 30 more Danes were recruited from Oconto, Wisconsin to colonize the settlement.

Though the developer W.C. Valentine named the city Modello, the Danes changed it to Dania in 1904.

Prosperous tomato farmers, the residents utilized the Florida East Coast Railway running through town to ship tomatoes to northern U.S. cities. Dania became known as "The Tomato Capital of the World," with carloads of tomatoes shipped to New Orleans for processing in a tomato paste factory. Tomato Day celebrations were held replete with a pageant queen and tomato fights.

Saltwater intrusion into the tomato fields put an end to the tomato boom in the late 1940's. Within 10 years, enterprising residents put Dania on the map as the "Antique Capital of the South."

Antique Row, located along Federal Highway, still exists. Here you can find all manner of treasures for purchase as well as historic architecture. From Art Deco at the Florida Theater to Mediterranean Revival at the Martin Frost House, to Greek Revival at the Dania Bank Building, there is a wealth of designs to explore.

If you're up for adventure, ask a local for directions to "Monkey Road." A colony of vervets, whose ancestors escaped from the Anthropoid Ape Research Foundation in the 1940's, live in an area lush with mangrove trees near the Fort Lauderdale airport.

In the 1990's locals would throw keg parties on Monkey Road, enjoying the antics of the monkeys as they picnicked.

For more information about Dania Beach check out www.daniabeachfl. gov.

CHULA

A chula is a perfect shot in Jai-Alai. Descended from the Basque game of pelota, the Jai Alai ball is the fastest moving ball of any sport, traveling at speeds of up to 188 mph. What is now the Dania Beach Casino was once home to a thriving fronton — the open-walled playing area where matches take place. An alternative to gambling on horses and greyhounds, the Miami and Dania Jai Alai frontons were once *the* place to be seen. Celebs such as Bob Hope, Babe Ruth and Ernest Hemingway enjoyed Jai Alai and when Don Shula, the winningest coach in NFL history visited, he was informed that the fans were shouting, "Chula!" not "Shula!" Like many gambling enterprises, the game was not without its share of shenanigans. A mob enforcer whacked the owner of Miami Jai Alai's parent firm in the early 1980's. A few years before that the Palm Beach Jai Alai was burned down by an arsonist suspected to have ties to organized crime. Nowadays you can catch Jai Alai at The Dania Beach Casino's Invitational tournament. Cheer on your favorite player with the word, "Chula," and shoot the perfect shot to go with it.

Ingredients

¾ shot Miami Club Cuban Coffee Liqueur
¼ shot Rum Chata

Directions

For best results chill the liqueurs beforehand. Layer a chilled shot glass with the coffee liqueur. Top with Rum Chata.

Tasting Notes

Though not always easy to find, Miami Club Cuban Coffee Liqueur is worth the search. It is bold, rich and well-balanced with an authentic Cuban coffee flavor.

RUMRUNNER

Rumrunners ran rampant on the Gold Coast during Prohibition. The combination of Florida's proximity to the Bahamas, where liqueur was legal, with our multitude of waterways created a perfect storm in which the bootleggers could ply their trade.

One such sweet spot is called Whiskey Creek Hideout. Whiskey Creek offered a multitude of places for small boats to hide, as the water was too shallow for policing vessels to pass through.

Rumor has it that the occasional antique whiskey or rum bottle still pops up from the creek bed. Locals love the birding, kayaking, canoe rentals and beautiful beach at Whiskey Creek.

Although the first Rumrunner cocktail wasn't created at Whiskey Creek, it is a fitting sip for such a storied place.

Ingredients

1 ounce light rum
1 ounce dark rum
1 ounce banana liqueur
1 ounce Chambord or blackberry brandy
1 ounce orange juice
1 ounce pineapple juice
Splash grenadine

Directions

Combine all ingredients in an ice-filled shaker. Shake vigorously. Strain into an ice-filled glass. Add a floater of high-proof rum, if desired. Garnish with a skewer of fresh fruit.

Tasting Notes

The traditional Rumrunner does not have the sweetness you will find in many of the frozen versions available on cruise ships and at bars. Taste and adjust sweetness to your palate accordingly.

Banana liqueurs wildly vary in smoothness and banana flavor. Giffard Banane du Brasil and Tempus Fugit Crème de Banana are two brands we recommend.

FENDER BENDER

One too many fender benders and you may think that those guitar strings reaching 20,000 feet into the sky or that ginormous 450-foot-tall guitar-shaped building you're seeing is a drunken apparition. You would be wrong.

It's the real McCoy. Owned by the Seminole Tribe of Florida, the hotel is designed to resemble back-to-back guitars and features floor-to-ceiling glass panels and brightly lit strings that change color depending on the season.

In addition to buying the Hard Rock brand in 2007, the Seminole Tribe facilitated the groundbreaking legal case that was the birth of modern commercial gambling on reservations.

While Fender is the foremost manufacturer of guitars, a Fender Bender is a simple cocktail consisting of 2/3 parts Yukon Jack, a honey-sweetened Canadian liqueur, and 1/3 part Cutty Sark.

Cutty Sark was the main product that Captain Bill McCoy smuggled into Florida and the United States during Prohibition. His whiskey wasn't diluted or altered, as was the cargo of other smugglers. This earned him the nickname, and us the expression, "The Real McCoy."

Ingredients

2/3 ounces Yukon Jack Liqueur
1/3 ounce Cutty Sark

Directions

Combine in a rocks glass filled with crushed ice. Serve.

Tasting Notes

Yukon Jack was originally sold as a liqueur and labeled "The Black Sheep of Canadian Liqueurs." It is not to be confused with 100 Proof Yukon Jack, which is labeled "Only the Strong Survive." The liqueur is blended with honey and is sweet with notes of citrus and spice.

MONKEY GLAND

The Monkey Gland cocktail was created during Prohibition, at Harry's Bar in Paris. While the U.S. was in the throes of Prohibition, people were drinking it up at Harry's. Dr. Serge Voronoff, a famous Parisian doctor, began transplanting monkey testicles into humans, supposedly to rejuvenate them. The thought of the procedure's aphrodisiac effect had no bearing on anything other than a cocktail being named in its honor.

Twenty years later, a group of vervet monkeys at Dania's Anthropoid Ape Research Foundation feared for their manhood. They successfully escaped the facility, creating a thriving colony in nearby mangrove trees.

The home of Dania novelist John Dufresne borders mangrove trees. Descendants of those wily escapees can frequently be found eating Dufresne's hibiscus and snacking on his wife Cindy's vegetable garden. Dufresne enjoys the monkeys so much that he has two monkeys named Alice and Bobby featured in his new book, *My Darling Boy*.

Ingredients

1 ½ ounce gin
1 ½ ounce freshly squeezed orange juice
1 teaspoon grenadine (preferably real pomegranate)
1 teaspoon absinthe or pastis
1 teaspoon simple syrup

Directions

Place all ingredients in an ice-filled shaker. Shake vigorously. Strain into a small, chilled cocktail glass.

ORANGE BLOSSOM CRUNCH

To celebrate National Orange Juice Day, Florida-based Tropicana created a honey almond breakfast cereal made specifically for orange juice instead of milk. Sadly it is almost impossible to find anymore.

Given the popularity of cereal-infused liquids in cocktails, swapping out the fresh oj in the classic orange blossom cocktail with cereal-infused oj seems a fun way to commemorate the orange groves that once thrived along the Gold Coast.

If you drive west along Dania Beach's Griffin Road, you may notice a massive mobile orange on the south side of the street. You are now in Davie, Florida, home of Bergeron Rodeo Grounds, the Orange Blossom Festival and parade, and Bob's Roth's New River Groves.

Right next to that giant orange is some of the best Florida citrus you will ever find. Founded in 1964, Bob Roth's New River Groves also sells what many believe to be the best Key lime pie in South Florida.

Ingredients

2 ounces gin
1 ounce Honey Bunches of Oats infused orange juice

Directions

Combine all ingredients in a shaker half-filled with ice. Strain into a chilled cocktail glass. Garnish with an orange wheel.

Cereal Infused Orange Juice

Pour a cup of cereal into a large glass and top with orange juice. Let steep for 20 minutes. Strain through a fine mesh strainer. Chill until ready to use.

Elevate

If you've never had a Honeybell orange, you're in for a treat. In season from mid-December to mid-February, Honeybells are tangelos. Tangelos are a hybrid of the Duncan grapefruit and the Dancy tangerine. They are sweet, juicy, seedless and easy to peel. For a tasty upgrade, swap out Honeybell juice in any recipe that orange juice is called for.

Everyone Under
the Sun

FORT LAUDERDALE

Fort Lauderdale was named for a trio of forts that were constructed by the U.S. military during the Second Seminole War, around 1838. The forts were named after Major William Lauderdale and his older brother, Lieutenant Colonel James Lauderdale.

Though none of the forts survived, the city continued to be a military hub with the WWII air station that trained thousands of pilots as well as radar and range finding schools. The Naval Air Station Fort Lauderdale is of note not just due to its military history, but it was also the likely origin of the Bermuda Triangle myth.

On December 5, 1945, five planes took off from the air station and were never seen again. The explosion of a search plane contributed to the mystery. Personal effects of the flight crew and models of the planes can be seen at the Naval Air Station Fort Lauderdale Museum.

Colgate University's swim team took their winter training to Fort Lauderdale in the 1930's, putting Lauderdale on the map as a spring break destination. With the publication of Glendon Swarthout's novel *Where the Boys Are,* and its subsequent movie, spring break was cemented. Fort Lauderdale began to be called Fort Liquordale.

The city shut down spring break shenanigans in the 1980's focusing on making the town a family-friendly destination. Attractions such as the Museum of Discovery & Science, pirate ship adventures, numerous beaches and parks are just a few of the city's fun family activities.

Though the nickname "Fort Liquorale" may no longer apply, we would be remiss if we didn't mention the abundance of quality bars, cocktail lounges and speakeasies that abound in Fort Lauderdale. Check out www.visitlauderdale.com for more information.

THE RAT TAKES THE CUP

Or should we say the cat takes the cup? In 2024 the Florida Panthers won the Stanley Cup for the first time! This shot is in honor of the team and the many loyal fans who have supported them through the years.

Why rat, you ask, when they are the Florida Panthers?

Back in 1995 the Panthers team captain, Scott Mellanby, smashed a rat in the Panther's dressing room using his hockey stick. That night he went on to score two goals which led to a player quipping, "He pulled a rat trick." The next night fans began throwing plastic rats onto the ice whenever the Panthers scored.

This shot is layered in the team's colors, red, blue and brown. Layered drinks work when the sugar content is highest in the bottom layer, then decreasing as you move upward. This is a very sweet shot. A little like the taste of victory.

Ingredients

¼ ounce maraschino cherry juice
½ ounce amaretto
1 drop blue food coloring
1 ounce vodka

Directions

Pour cherry juice into the bottom of a chilled shot glass. Carefully add amaretto. Add the drop of food coloring into the vodka and thoroughly combine. Gently pour on top of the amaretto.

SPICY AVOCADO MARGARITA

During the fall our neighbors up north are enjoying apple picking. Here on the Gold Coast, we're picking avocados. Because a single tree can produce as many as 500 avocados per year, the lucky Floridians who have a tree in their yard share their wealth with friends and family throughout the season.

An Aztec symbol of love and lust, the avocado was considered to be such an aphrodisiac that some maidens were kept inside during the growing season so they could resist temptation.

Many of our fair young maidens can be found sunning themselves on the beaches of Fort Lauderdale or enjoying a tipple at trendy spots such as Lona Cocina Tequileria.

The following is their recipe for a spicy avocado margarita. Although excellent with tacos or other Mexican foods, this spicy avocado margarita is the perfect temptation to offer for brunch. Consider mixing up a pitcher for ease of service.

Ingredients

2 ounces Ghost Tequila
½ ounce lime juice
½ ounce agave
1 tablespoon pureed avocado
1 slice jalapeno

Directions

Combine tequila, lime juice, agave and avocado puree in an ice-filled shaker. Strain into a chilled, ice-filled margarita glass. Garnish with a slice of jalapeno.

Tasting Notes

Ghost Tequila is made with a hint of ghost pepper, the third-highest pepper on the Scoville scale of spiciness. The tequila delivers a quick hit of heat followed by a smooth, fruity finish.

FLORIDA OLD FASHIONED

What could be better than shining a spotlight on Fort Lauderdale's restaurants, hotels, chefs and mixologists via the week-long Visit Lauderdale Food and Wine Festival? A week-long festival that benefits the Joe DiMaggio Children's Hospital.

Not only has the hospital succeeded in providing world-class medical care to both the rich and poor in our community, but it has earned 4 out of 4 stars in its rating among non-profit organizations. That's pretty impressive. Also impressive is the lineup of stars who generously give of their time and energy to benefit the hospital.

One such person is celebrity chef, Nancy Fuller. Chef Nancy is host of the Food Network series, *Farmhouse Rules*. Author of the cookbook, *Farmhouse Rules*, Nancy created her own bourbon, GG Guice.

This luscious sip is perfect in the cocktail Nancy created for one of the festival's fundraising dinners.

While traditional old fashions are made with bitters and sweetened with simple syrup, this one is made with local honey and one of our favorite local fruits – guava.

Easy to make, this cocktail is great to batch prepare for parties or celebrations.

Ingredients

2 ounces GG Guice Bourbon
1 ounce Florida honey syrup
Splash of guava nectar

Directions

Stir or shake all ingredients. Pour into a chilled, ice-filled glass. Garnish with an orange slice, peel, or whatever your heart desires!

Florida Honey Syrup

½ cup Florida honey
½ cup sugar
1 cup water

Directions

Bring everything to a boil in a small saucepan. Cool before use.

ANTHONY'S PAPER PLANE

Rumors swirl that Runway 84, the red sauce joint up the road from Fort Lauderdale International Airport was once the meeting place of mafiosi in the 80's and 90's. We can neither confirm nor deny.

What we can tell you is that the dark, clubby restaurant interior has been redesigned to feel like the Copacabana nightclub scene from the movie *Goodfellas*, replete with candlelit tables, live music and a storied guest list including luminaries such as Al Pacino, William H. Macy, Dan Marino, Evander Holyfield and more.

The Paper Plane served here is named for one of the owners, Anthony, and tweaked with passion fruit — one of our most beloved ingredients in South Florida.

Ingredients

1 ½ ounces Russels Bourbon
½ ounce Amaro Nonino
½ ounce Aperol
¼ ounce passion fruit puree
¼ ounce freshly squeezed lemon juice

Directions

Add all ingredients into an ice-filled shaker. Shake vigorously. Strain into a coupe glass. Garnish with a dehydrated orange.

STACEY'S FAVORITE PUNCH

My sister Stacey loves punches. Not the kind I used to give her as a kid, but the fruity, sweet and sometimes slushy punches that you find served in hurricane glasses, fish bowls and aquariums. Yes – there are pictures of Stacey drinking from both fish bowls and aquariums.

There are places in Fort Lauderdale known to serve tiki drinks from fish bowls as well. While I'm not opposed to drinking from an aquarium or fish bowl, I will admit to being partial to serving punch at parties. I like to use a pretty drink dispenser placed on a table near the front door. That way people can grab a drink on the way in and make their way to the bar and their favorite pour later.

The Wilder bar in Fort Lauderdale holds a burlesque brunch during which a Garden Punch Bowl is offered. Featuring Ketel One Peach & Orange Blossom Botanicals, it is served in an old-school crystal punch bowl with dainty cups.

Stacey's Favorite Punch is a peachy version of my sister's classic frozen punch recipe. Bust out the crystal bowl and cute cups for your next party, fill up a gorgeous drink dispenser, or use a few drops of blue food coloring and ladle this into a fish bowl with some skewered gummy fish for garnish. Whatever you choose we won't judge.

Ingredients

1 750 ml bottle Ketel One Botanical Peach & Orange Blossom Vodka

1 52-ounce bottle Simply Peach Juice Drink

1 12-ounce can frozen lemonade concentrate

6 cups water

1 bottle prosecco or champagne

Directions

Mix all ingredients except for the lemon-lime soda in a large bowl. Ladle into gallon size zip top bags until about half full. Freeze.

Defrost bags of frozen punch prior to serving. Place in a punch bowl and break up with a fork if necessary. Top with sparkling wine.

POMPANO BEACH

Legend has it that Pompano Beach was named after a tasty dinner of Pompano fish. Railroad employee Frank Sheen noted the local fish on a survey map. The name stuck and was formally called Pompano when the city incorporated in 1947.

Home to a 1,000-foot-long municipal fishing pier, Pompano Beach is home to many fishing tournaments as well as offshore live coral reefs. The SS Copenhagen shipwreck is located on the Pompano Dropoff reef, about three-quarters of a nautical mile offshore of Lauderdale-by-the-Sea. Used as target practice by the U.S. Navy during WWII, the site has been declared a Florida Underwater Archaeological Preserve and remains a popular dive spot.

The Festival Marketplace and Hillsboro Antique Mall are popular Pompano shopping destinations. Festival Marketplace spans over a quarter mile from end to end and is renowned for its discounted prices. The Hillsboro Antique Mall boasts over 200 individual booths selling unique antiques and collectibles.

Music Under the Stars is a popular activity provided by the city on Pompano Beaches Great Lawn. There is a quarterly newsletter listing many local activities that can be downloaded at www.pompanobeachfl. gov.

PASSION FRUIT BATIDA

It stands to reason that Itajai, Brazil would be a sister city to Pompano Beach. Pompano is home to what is considered the largest population of Brazilians in South Florida.

Take a drive along Sample Road and you will find a fabulous array of Brazilian and Portuguese specialty food shops, restaurants and bakeries. Try a brigadeiro, one of the best loved candies in Brazil. Made from condensed milk and chocolate, brigadeiros are synonymous with fun.

Also made with condensed milk and synonymous with fun is the Brazilian drink called batida.

Batida means shaken or milkshake. Thick and creamy, batidas are commonly served in Brazil at Carnival, family parties and beachside.

Once eschewed by upscale bars and restaurants because of their sweetness, batidas have been re-introduced by some mixologists without condensed milk. Feel free to substitute simple syrup if you're not a fan of condensed milk.

Ingredients

¼ cup diced passion fruit
½ tablespoon condensed milk
1 ounce cachaca
¼ cup ice

Directions

Add all ingredients to the blender and blitz until smooth. Pour into a chilled glass.

Tasting Notes

Batidas can be made with almost any fruit you like. Fresh fruits which are about to turn are excellent choices to freeze. Cut into small cubes and freeze in a zip top bag.

SHIP SANK SANGRIA

One man's sludge tanker is another man's treasure.

Located in Ship Wreck Park, one mile SE of the Hillsboro Inlet in Pompano Beach is one of Florida's largest artificial reefs.

In its former life, the Newton Creek moved sewage from facilities in New York to places that would convert the sludge into fertilizer pellets. Not a glamorous job, but a necessary one.

After fifty years of noble service, the Newton Creek was put up for auction and purchased by Ship Wreck Park. This was thanks to donations from Isle Casino Racing and the City of Pompano Beach.

Before it was sunk to the depth of 126 ft., the Newtown Creek was reborn as The Lady Luck. Outfitted to be the world's first underwater casino, artist Dennis McDonald created life size octopus dealers, slot machines and literal card sharks on deck.

We've all heard the expression, "He stepped in s***," meaning he was blessed with blind luck. Whether that translates to swimming aboard The Lady Luck we have no clue. Could the Newton Creek's reincarnation be a kind of karmic nirvana? Quite possibly so.

Ingredients

1 ounce Malibu Passion Fruit
1 ounce Peach Schnapps
2 ounces passion fruit juice
2 ounces orange juice
2 ounces lemonade
2 ounces prosecco

Directions

Combine all ingredients except for prosecco in an ice-filled shaker. Shake vigorously. Strain into a chilled hurricane glass filled with crushed ice. Top with prosecco. Garnish with an orange slice, lemon slice and a cherry.

SOREL SPARKLER

Before Kool-Aid, there was sorrel. The Caribbean name for hibiscus flowers, recipes for medicinal and aromatic drinks made from sorrel were brought to North America by enslaved Africans.

The original "red drink," sorrel recipes vary from family to family and island to island. Jamaican sorrel was frequently flavored with ginger and five spice, while Trinidad and Tobago's version contained clove, nutmeg and cinnamon.

Africans from the Bahamas were some of the first settlers in Pompano Beach. There you can find the Ali Cultural Arts Center, an 87-year-old building that was once the home of Frank and Florence Major Ali, the first African American business owners in Pompano.

Pompano Beach celebrates Juneteenth, also called Freedom or Emancipation Day, with a Blues and Sweet Potato Pie Festival. During the festival the best sweet potato pie maker is crowned. The Sorel sparkler would be a fitting drink with which to toast the winner.

Our Sorel sparkler is spelled with one "r" as a primary ingredient is Sorel liqueur, as opposed to sorrel tea.

Ingredients

1 ounce gin
1 ½ ounce Sorel liqueur
3 ounces Champagne or dry sparkling wine

Directions

Combine gin and Sorel in an ice-filled shaker. Shake vigorously and strain into a chilled Champagne flute. Top with Champagne or sparkling wine. Garnish with a long lemon strip.

Notes

Created by Jackie Summers, Sorel is a liqueur inspired by the original sorrel and with a recipe passed down from his grandparents. Sorel blends many botanicals and spices for its signature taste.

PERFECT STORM

The term perfect storm has been used in a multitude of ways. Back in 1850 the Rev. Lloyd of Withington used the expression in a meteorological sense. Perfect storm is used in psychological theory and is considered synonymous with the "worst-case scenario."

It is also the title of a popular book by creative nonfiction writer Sebastian Junger.

On a more pleasant note, a perfect storm is sometimes used to describe romantic love — serendipitous or fortuitous circumstances that result in a positive outcome.

Such is the case with the perfect storm cocktail. A classic summer cocktail descended from the Dark 'n Stormy, the Perfect Storm can be tweaked and varied to suit your taste.

Ingredients

½ ounce strawberry syrup
1 ounce Captain Morgan
1 ounce Bacardi white
1 ounce cranberry juice
1 ounce lime

Directions

Shake and strain. Rosemary sprig and cinnamon stick garnish.

COQUITO

Once called, "Miami's nuttiest tourist bait," coconuts were distributed at the 1962 Seattle's World Fair, handed to disembarking passengers at Fort Lauderdale's Port Everglades, provided as prizes from a Rotary club, gifted to children by singing mailmen and given away at Yankee Stadium during the Gotham Bowl Game.

Puerto Rican people know that everyone loves a little taste of the tropics, just as our neighbors from P.R. know that coconut is a tasty base for their most beloved holiday libation.

Translated to little coconut, coquito was originally a holiday beverage meant to be gifted and shared. Our version is for a large batch and though it's the traditional basic flavor, tastes far from basic. Enjoy as is or use it as a jumping-off point to create your own holiday flavor.

Ingredients

3 cinnamon sticks
2 cups water
1 can coconut milk
1 can cream of coconut

1 can evaporated milk
1 cup white rum
1 cup spiced rum
1 teaspoon vanilla

Directions

Boil the cinnamon sticks in the water until the water turns yellowish and smells like cinnamon. Remove the sticks and let cool.

Combine the cinnamon "tea" with the remaining ingredients in a blender. Pulse until thoroughly combined. Pour into glass bottles or quart jars and refrigerate.

Garnish with a sugar rim and cinnamon stick.

Makes 8-10 servings

A City for
All Seasons

BOCA RATON

The road to Boca Raton was inspired by the Botofogo in Rio de Janiero, Brazil. Architect and dreamer Addison Cairns Mizner envisioned a grand resort community in Boca Raton, with an entrance that was to be one of the finest in North America.

While not as grand as Mizner hoped, the palm-lined street Camino Real stands today as the entrance to the luxurious Boca Raton Resort and Club.

Known for its affluence and outrageous displays of wealth, Boca Raton is one of the richest and most educated cities in Palm Beach County.

Here you can indulge in your wildest crazy rich fantasies. Care for a bottle of 2003 Chateau Lafite Roschild 1er Grand Cru Classe? It can be yours at Abe & Louie's restaurant.

How about a redflower hammam spa treatment with champagne, mini-cupcakes, rubber duckies, submersion in a heated float bed while being slathered in a phyto-power sea mask, cooled with an orange quince mist and finished with a warm cardamom oil and tangerine fig butter crème massage? After that you can get your toes done on a custom pedicure throne.

Alternatively, you could enjoy free entry to Boca's Gumbo Limbo Nature Center, across from the beach and Red Reef Park. In addition to being a rescue facility for injured sea turtles, the center has an open-air butterfly garden, nature trail, lighted outdoor aquariums and gorgeous sunset views over the Intracoastal Waterway.

Since 1977 the city has employed a Sea Turtle Conservation team and Gumbo Limbo holds nesting walks and hatchling releases as well as education and community outreach programs.

In 2023 alone the nature center recorded 1,277 sea turtle nests on a 5-mile stretch of Boca's beach. The types of turtle you may come across are Leatherback, Loggerhead and Green.

The recreation services department at the city has a jam-packed schedule of free activities you can partake of while visiting the area. Check out The Recreator publication for the latest calendar of events. It can be found at www.myboca.us.

WHAT A WONDERFUL WORLD CAIPIRINHA

Addison Mizner said, "Exaggeration is unessential. The future of Boca Raton is far too opulent to require coloring."

Perhaps the best-known architect of his time, Mizner designed stunning Mediterranean Revival and Spanish Colonial Revival mansions for the wealthy socialites of Palm Beach.

He saw the potential in Boca Raton, a small unincorporated farming town established in 1896. Embarking on what he considered to be his culminating achievement, Mizner gathered investors, became the city's first planner, and forged ahead.

Part of Mizner's strategy included hosting a daily cocktail party at 5 o'clock for friends and potential clients. His normal breakfast in bed included a split of champagne and pitcher of fresh-squeezed orange juice, delivered by the butler.

He was also known to enjoy rum cocktails served in antique silver cups. Because Mizner modeled Boca's main street after the Botofogo in Brazil, we wonder if cachaca, Brazil's national spirit, was part of his repertoire?

Distilled from the fermented juice of fresh sugar cane, cachaca is the third most widely consumed spirit in the world. Channel Mizner with this traditional capirinha by serving it in an antique silver cup. Put on some Louis Armstrong, one of Mizner's favorite musicians, and savor the moment. No coloring required.

Ingredients

1 lime cut into wedges	2 ½ ounces cachaca
2 teaspoons superfine sugar	Lime wheel

Directions

Muddle lime and sugar at the bottom of a chilled, antique sterling silver cup. Fill with ice. Add cachaca and stir well. Garnish with a lime wheel.

ARNOLD PALMER SMASH

Smash factor in golf is your club head speed divided by your ball speed. It is a measure of efficiency.

A Smash In cocktail is a member of the Mint Julep family. A Mint Julep is stirred while a Smash is aggressively smashed and shaken. Historically the Smash also lacked the flash of the Mint Julep's cups, metal straws and Derby hats. It is, in effect, a more effective Mint Julep.

Modern Smashes often include muddled fruit, citrus and sometimes herb swaps.

This Smash is a nod to golf great, Arnold Palmer, and the fresh strawberries that thrive on the Gold Coast. Palmer is credited with creating the iced tea and lemonade drink known as Arnold Palmer. Boca Raton is renowned for its world class golf courses, one of which is the stunning Arnold Palmer course at the St. Andrews Country Club.

Ingredients

5 frozen strawberries, slightly thawed
2 teaspoons sugar
5 mint leaves
One tablespoon fresh lime juice
1 ½ ounces Woodford
1 ½ ounces lemonade
1 ½ ounces cold brewed tea

Directions

Muddle the strawberries with the sugar in a chilled Collins glass. Add the remaining ingredients to an ice-filled shaker and shake vigorously. Strain into the rocks glass and gently stir. Garnish with fresh mint and a strawberry.

Tasting Notes

Swap out strawberries for your favorite fruit here. Also, consider brewing a flavored tea such as Earl Grey for a twist.

AI PAPI DOUBLE

There are many ways to say, "Ai papi!" If you listen closely, you will hear the phrase used in its multiple meanings all over South Florida.

Translating to "oh, daddy" as opposed to "oh, papa," ai papi can be said in a playful, flirtatious, or sexy way from a woman to her man. It can also be said in a disappointing tone. "Ai, papi," when a little boy disappoints his mom, right before she launches a chancleta at him.

The Gold Coast's most beloved papi, Ernest Hemingway, hated his first name. He chose the nickname "Papa" for himself and though he had many other nicknames, this was his favorite.

Another favorite of Hemingway's is the Hemingway Daiquiri, also called the Papa Double.

We've switched it up a little here, swapping in Key lime juice for the Persian lime juice it's normally made with. And while Hemingway was not a fan of sugar in his daiquiri, we beg to differ.

Ingredients

3 ounces blanco rum
1 ounce freshly squeezed pink grapefruit juice
¾ ounce Luxardo
1 ounce Key lime juice
½ ounce rich simple syrup

Directions

Shake in an ice-filled shaker. Strain into a chilled coupe glass. Garnish with a lime wheel or grapefruit twist

FLORIDA HEAT

The Florida Heat cocktail was created by mixologist John Kao. John laughingly refers to himself as an intoxicologist as he explains the thought process behind the drink's origination.

Created as an ode to the team at Steel Tie Distillery, John wanted a cocktail that would be indicative of South Florida's climate. A nod to both our basketball team and the weather, Florida Heat utilizes spice to help cool down the body.

The active compound in chili peppers is called capsaicin. Capsaicin triggers sweat without raising your body temperature, which helps to cool the body naturally.

Dehydrated sweet peppers were chosen to garnish the drink because they have a longer shelf life in humid weather and they also float. Because the fruit purees in the cocktail already contain sugars, John only adds a touch of agave to sweeten. As a rule, you can use less agave than sugar when building a cocktail to achieve the same level of sweetness.

John says the order in which you build is important, too. Begin with the cheapest, most viscous liquid and go from there. Ice is always last and is important when considering not just chilling but dilution.

Finally, when creating drinks, think about the harmony between what you're drinking and what you'll be eating. Pairings are not only important but flavor profiles can be carried across both fronts.

One of John's favorite dishes consists of pork braised in a reduction of the Miami Heat cocktail.

Ingredients

1 ½ ounces Steel Tie Habanero Vodka
½ ounce agave
¼ ounce freshly squeezed lime juice
½ ounce peach puree
½ ounce mango puree

Directions

Shake all ingredients in an ice-filled shaker. Double strain into a chilled coupe glass. Garnish with skewered sweet pepper rings and a basil sprig.

WAKE THE DEAD

If Florida Man were to build an amusement park, he might build it on a 24-acre Indian burial mound in Boca Raton. There he would tunnel into the mound and set windows into the soil, allowing visitors to see into the grave sites.

He would also include artifacts from the Spanish conquest of Florida such as ship cannons and anchors — items that contributed to the complete annihilation of the Tequesta tribe that once inhabited the area.

This scenario did, of course, take place. The amusement park was called Ancient America and operated from 1953-1958.

A place such as this brings to mind scenes from the 1982 film *Poltergeist*, in which bad things happen to a family because their house is built on a cemetery.

We can't be sure if any children were kidnapped by poltergeists when the park was operational, but we can report that it failed. The site was purchased by developers who built the Boca Marina Yacht Club.

Portions of the mound are still visible from the front entrance of the high-end, luxurious gated community. It is now named The Sanctuary.

The Sanctuary's newest resident is Billy Joel. He just bought a home there for $29 million. Welcome to the neighborhood, Billy.

Ingredients

1 ounce blanco tequila
1 ounce coffee liqueur
½ ounce espresso

Directions

Pour all ingredients into an ice-filled shaker. Shake vigorously. Strain into a chilled shot glass.

Village By the Sea

DELRAY BEACH

Prior to turning pro, Venus and Serena Williams trained almost anywhere a court could be found in Delray Beach. Not only is the local weather conducive to tennis, but local residents and the city government have made strides to grow the sport locally since 1992.

Home to The Delray Beach Open, the city also boasts a hotspot for some of the sport's best players at The Delray Beach Tennis Center.

Downtown Delray celebrates the city's vibrant art scene with First Friday Art Walks and the Delray Beach Art Trail. The city takes art seriously, with a variety of museums and locations dedicated to preserving and sharing African-American history, as well as Japanese cultural history, architectural styles and galleries, including one inside a city parking garage.

In the mid-1920's an Artists and Writers Colony was established in Delray along with the adjacent town of Gulf Stream. By the 1930's and 1940's Delray had become a popular winter retreat for many artists and writers. Luminaries such as Edna St. Vincent Millay and cartoonists H.T. Webster and Fontaine Fox gathered over the Arcade Tap Room located in the Arcade Building.

The Arcade Building was designed by Samuel Ogren Sr., the father of Delray architecture. Delray's Sandoway House as well as the 1926 high school and gymnasium at Old School Square are other examples of Ogren's work that can be enjoyed during a visit to Delray.

Additional Delray Beach cultural events and places of interest can be found at www.downtowndelraybeach.com.

ORANGE GROVE HOUSE OF REFUGE

Before we had a Coast Guard, there was a US Lifesaving Service. With roots in 18th century volunteer efforts in Massachusetts, the Service was formed to save the lives of shipwrecked mariners and passengers.

Five houses were built by the Service along Florida's coast, one of which was in Delray Beach. Called the Orange Grove House of Refuge, it was named for a rock wall that was likely built during an early Spanish settlement. Located two blocks north of Atlantic Avenue on North Ocean Boulevard, an acre of wild oranges grew near the site.

Ponce de Leon is credited with bringing oranges to the New World during his 1513 journey. As opposed to popular myth, de Leon didn't land here looking for a fountain of youth. He was looking for gold and adventure.

Besides housing shipwrecked sailors, the Orange Grove House of Refuge served as an overnight shelter for the Barefoot Mailmen on their journey up and down the beaches. It also housed pioneers in search of the same gold and adventure that de Leon sought.

At a cost of $2 to $3 a month, the pioneers had access to the cots and bedding that were kept in constant readiness for shipwrecked mariners. As of August, 2024, the median home price in Delray Beach was $474,500. The average monthly rent there is $2,823.00. Gold hunt indeed.

Ingredients

1 pineapple spear
1 stalk rosemary
1 ounce gin
1 ounce orange juice
¼ ounce lime juice
1 ounce water

Directions

Muddle the pineapple and rosemary at the bottom of a shaker. Fill halfway with ice and add the remaining ingredients. Shake vigorously and strain into an ice-filled cocktail glass. Garnish with pineapple leaves and orange slices.

BAREFOOT MAILMAN

Neither tropical storms nor heat nor hurricanes stays our couriers from the swift completion of their appointed rounds.

The Greek historian Herodotus said something similar referring to the messengers of the Persian Empire. About 2,400 years later, the Barefoot Mailmen arrived in Florida. From the years 1885-1893 there wasn't a road connecting the 68-mile route from Palm Beach to Miami. The mailmen walked along the sand and traveled by boat to make their deliveries to grateful pioneers.

The mailmen's first stop for the night took place at Delray Beaches Orange Grove House of Refuge. If you take a walk along A1A, you'll find a placard marking the spot where the Grosvenor House Condominium now stands.

To honor the legacy of the Barefoot Mailmen, a 35-mile hike is reenacted every year by the Boy Scouts of America. Carrying a mailbag, the scouts begin in Pompano Beach and end in Miami Beach.

Ingredients

1½ ounces white rum
½ ounce lime juice
1 teaspoon maraschino cherry juice
½ ounce oregat

Directions

Rim a chilled cocktail glass with tajin spice, if desired. Add the rum, lime juice, maraschino cherry juice and oregat into an ice-filled shaker. Shake and strain into the rimmed glass. Garnish with a lime wheel.

BOOZY STRAWBERRY SHAKE

Strawberry shakes have been a South Florida favorite since the 1950's. From Knaus Berry Farm in the Redlands to The Girls Strawberry U-Pick in Delray, you can cool off during our warm winter months with a handmade frozen treat.

Though some of our local strawberry farms were shuttered due to development, The Girls remains a sweet spot for nostalgia.

Run by the same family that owns The Boys Farmers Market, Bambini's Pizza and Gramma's Bakery, The Girls is a beacon for family fun. Though they no longer offer berry picking, kids of all ages enjoy the petting zoo, swans and exotic birds out back.

Old-school candy is sold indoors, along with homemade ice cream. Bambini's Pizza is connected so you can grab a New York-style slice before your animal encounter and then a banana split after.

Go to Gramma's Bakery, just a few feet away, for tomorrow's bread, pies, cookies or cakes.

Alternatively, bring home a pint of The Girls's ice cream and some fresh strawberries for your own homemade treat. Though we are partial to bourbon in our shakes, you can substitute with whatever spirit is your favorite.

Ingredients

1 ½ ounces bourbon
1 cup vanilla ice cream
6 frozen strawberries
½ cup milk

Directions

Combine all ingredients in a blender. Blitz until smooth and frothy. Serve in a chilled glass with a straw and a strawberry.

Elevate

Chunk over ripe bananas into one-inch sections and freeze in zip-top bags for banana shakes. Add banana liqueur to change things up. Top with whipped cream, a cherry, chocolate syrup and sprinkles for special occasions.

TRAIN WRECKED

Trouble abounds in one Delray Beach area. Neighbors are at odds regarding the harems and parties roaming the streets at all hours, damaging cars, jumping from trees to rooftops and making all manner of annoying noises.

Male vasectomies have provided relief in other Florida towns facing the same issue.

We are talking about peacocks and peahens, of course. Not native to Florida, this invasive species arrived as lawn ornaments for affluent homeowners in the 1920's.

Peacocks — the males — make a gorgeous fan of color around their bodies with the feathers called a train. This both attracts females and makes them appear larger to deter predators.

Originating from the Indian subcontinent, peafowl represent royalty and power, immortality, wisdom, and fearlessness from serpents.

Peafowl are present all around the Gold Coast. You may spot them roaming around residential neighborhoods, during tours at fabulous facilities such as Flamingo Gardens in Davie or Holiday Park Everglades.

Whether you consider them a nuisance or delight, peafowl are here to stay. They are protected by law. Rather than castrate them, some residents plant flowers that deter peafowl such as hibiscus or prickly pear cactus.

The smartest residents utilize both the prickly pear and hibiscus in cocktails. Win/win.

Ingredients

1 ounce tequila
½ ounce Sorel hibiscus liqueur
1 ounce prickly pear syrup
2 ounces hibiscus tea
Squeeze of lime

Directions

Fill a chilled cocktail glass ¾ the way full of ice. Add Sorel and a squeeze of lime. Top with ginger beer. Garnish with a lime twist.

PINEAPPLE PARADISE

Pineapples play a large part in both the history of Delray Beach and the city as we now know it. Pineapples were the most well-known crop in Delray for decades, both commercially and residentially. Many families were farmers and others kept small pineapple patches in their yards.

Although disease and the prevalence of east coast pineapple crops saw the pineapple plants disappear, the fruit remained. There is an arts district in downtown Delray called the Pineapple Grove Arts District as well as a mural called "Pineapple Paradise" on the side of the Chloe Building on East Atlantic Avenue. This mural replaced a water damaged mural called "Dancing Pineapples" by Anita Lovitt.

To make your pineapple dance, pair it with Florida basil. Preferably with the Florida Basil Vodka made by ChainBridge Distillery. Located in nearby Oakland Park, ChainBridge infuses two types of fresh basil grown on Florida farms into their craft vodka.

A popular drink in the 1980's, spritzes have made a comeback. Spritzes are, in fact, one of the most ordered cocktails today.

Ingredients

¼ cup fresh pineapple juice
1 ounce lime juice
2 ounces Florida Basil Vodka
4 ounces sparkling water

Directions

Add pineapple juice, lime juice and vodka to an ice-filled shaker. Shake vigorously. Strain into an ice-filled glass. Top with sparkling water. Garnish with fresh pineapple and pineapple leaves.

America's Gateway
to the Gulfstream

BOYNTON BEACH

Boynton Beach was founded in 1898 by Fred S. Dewey, a secretary to Henry Flagler. Along with his wife Byrd, Dewey purchased a large tract of land west of the Intracoastal Waterway and filed the original plat in the Dade County courthouse.

Committed to the preservation of history, the City of Boynton Beach Heritage Education program boasts three interactive maps on its website: a Black history interactive map;highlighting contributions made to the city by Black residents; a heritage trail map that is 1.5 miles long and includes 30 sites of historical interest; and a historic site map that details over 170 significant sites within the city.

Tales of pirates, hidden treasure and lost caves abound in both Boynton and Delray Beaches, with archaeological evidence proving that a system of rocky outcroppings and underground caverns once were visible in today's Gulf Stream (south of Gulf Stream Beach).

The caves provided a hideout for Confederate soldiers, playground for local youths and motorcycle gangs, as well as a place of refuge for the Barefoot Mailmen. Delray author W.J. Pat Enright immortalized the caves and coined the name Sailor Jim's Cave in the book by the same name about a mystery of buried treasure in Florida. Download the book for free at www.archive.org.

LADYBUG LANDING

Pumpkin patches, fall festivals, corn mazes and sunflower fields are just some of the family activities you'll find at Bedner's Farm. Here they have a fantastic selection of luscious fruits and vegetables from which to choose, as well as seasonal U-pick activities, tractor rides, a petting zoo, and a butterfly and ladybug park.

Not only do ladybugs like to land on plants, but they are a beneficial predator that can eat up to 5,000 aphids in their lifetime. This is good news for the cucumbers that flourish at Bedner's farm. Fewer aphids = more cucumbers for your cocktails.

If you've never tried cucumbers in cocktails before, you're missing out. Here we've combined pineapple and cucumber along with mango-flavored sparkling water to help you cool off after a day of laboring in the U-pick fields.

And though the ladybugs are great for the cucumber plants and pretty to look at, proceed with caution. When threatened, ladybugs bite!

Ingredients

1 1-inch cucumber round, cut in half and then quartered
2 ounces Pineapple Malibu
1 ounce pineapple simple syrup
3 ounces mango flavored sparkling water
Pineapple spear and pineapple leaf to garnish

Directions

Muddle the cucumber at the bottom of a shaker tin. Add Pineapple Malibu and simple syrup. Fill shaker halfway with ice. Shake vigorously. Strain into an ice-filled hi-ball glass. Add sparkling water and give a gentle stir with a bar spoon. Garnish with a pineapple spear and pineapple leaf.

*Try rimming half of the glass with Tajin for a spicy note.

Pineapple Simple Syrup

1 cup granulated sugar
1 cup water
1 cup diced pineapple

Directions

Combine all
ingredients in a
small saucepan. Bring
to a boil on high heat.
Give a stir and reduce
heat to low. Simmer for 30
minutes. Strain through a fine
mesh sieve. Cool and store in a
glass jar in the refrigerator.

Keeps for two months in the
refrigerator if tightly sealed.

**The fruits, simple syrups, and
flavored sparkling waters can be
mixed and matched with whatever
flavors interest you. For example,
swap out strawberry simple syrup
for the pineapple simple syrup and
strawberry lemon sparkling water
for the mango flavor.

GiGi REFRESHER

Boynton Beach is a treasure trove for nature lovers. Catch the sunrise on the beach and then head west for a hike before the stunning sunset.

Green Cay Wetlands, the Arthur R. Marshall Loxahatchee National Wildlife Refuge and Ocean Ridge Hammock Park are just a few of the places where you can walk along boardwalks or easy trails to spot the bounty of wildlife and native plants that call Boynton home.

Alligators, of course, abound. But this area is also a birder's paradise. Here you may spot roseate spoonbills, great blue herons, pileated woodpeckers, sandhill cranes, wood storks (threatened), snail kites (endangered), and many more.

Alcohol is not allowed in most of the refuges, but don't fret. We have the perfect sip to pack in your picnic hamper.

Local mixologist GiGi Colombo first created this drink first as a mocktail. Strawberries, mint and lemon blend beautifully to provide a thirst-quenching sip that isn't overly sweet.

Ingredients

3 strawberries, stems removed
6 mint leaves
1 ½ ounces lemonade (or Haku vodka for the boozy version)
3 ounces Sprite

Directions

Muddle the strawberries and mint in the bottom of a shaker. Add the lemonade or vodka. Shake vigorously. Pour into a chilled, ice-filled Collins glass. Top with Sprite. Garnish with mint leaves and sliced strawberries.

Tasting Notes

Haku vodka is rice-based, and as such lends a subtle sweetness and smoothness to the finished product. GiGi chose it for this drink because of its clean taste.

FLYING CHANCLETA

Fwa-ka-ta is the sound a chancleta (flip flop) makes when it sails through the air and connects with its human target. My kids were introduced to flying flip flops by their beloved babysitter, Rosie. Rosie was a lousy shot and her attempts at fwakataing them were met by giggles as they ran away.

My friend Jessie was not so lucky. Her mom had great aim. Jessie's trauma from the flying chanclas is real, people. So much so that she's thinking about starting a nonprofit called Cancel Chancla Culture.

As gin is her favorite spirit, she's proposed that all CCC meetings begin with a gin cocktail. Rosie heard about it and insists that the drink include Seco, the crystal clear rum that's the national spirit of her native country, Panama. Finish the drink with a bamboo flip flop stirrer and say cheers to our new chancleta culture: throw back a drink rather than throwing a shoe at your kid.

Ingredients

1 ½ ounces Seco Herrerano
1 ounce gin
½ ounce fresh lime juice
½ ounce simple syrup
Ginger beer

Directions

Combine Seco, gin, lime juice and simple syrup in an ice-filled shaker. Shake vigorously and strain into an ice-filled cocktail glass. Top with ginger beer. Garnish with a flip flop stirrer and a lime wheel.

Tasting Notes

Seco is a clear, high-proof version of rum. Seco Herrerano is the most popular and readily available brand. It is neutral and dry, with fruity notes and a little sweetness. If Seco isn't readily available in your area, a neutral vodka or rum is a good substitute.

MANGO COSMO

Mangoes are synonymous with the Gold Coast. First carried by pirates around South Florida, the seeds were discarded, producing trees in Key West. The most popular variety grown in Florida prior to World War II came from the garden of Mrs. Florence Haden. A combination of Mulgoba mango from India and the Turpentine variety from the Caribbean, the Haden has excellent flavor and pretty red, yellow and green colors.

Florida mangoes are so beloved that some residents put caution tape and warning signs around their trees, prohibiting passersby from plucking the sweet fruit. Other Floridians are generous, clipping bags to their fences so that anyone who is inclined can enjoy a mango.

Back when the Gold Coast was still primarily a vacation destination, a group of chefs were inspired by local ingredients. Led by chefs Allen Susser, Mark Norman Van Aken, Douglas Rodriguez and Mark Militello, they became known as The Mango Gang. Their trailblazing cuisine helped define South Florida's distinct culinary identity.

Multiple mango festivals can be enjoyed all around the Gold Coast during harvest season in July. Check out Fairchild Tropical Garden and the Island Space Caribbean Museum in Plantation for information. Home to over 3,000 species of plants, Flamingo Gardens in Davie is a great place to check out mango trees. Here you can take a ride on the tram and tour lush, wandering paths.

Ingredients

1 ounce Shady Vodka
1 ounce cranberry juice
½ ounce Mango Chinola
½ ounce fresh lime juice

Directions

Combine all ingredients in an ice-filled shaker. Strain into a chilled martini glass. Garnish with mango.

Tasting Notes

Shady Vodka is distilled in Fort Lauderdale. Made from corn, Shady is distilled 7 times and contains no sweeteners. It is carb-free and has a smooth finish.

Chinola Mango is a natural, low ABV liqueur made with 100% fresh mango and no artificial flavors. It is crafted from a blend of Keitt, Kent and Banilejo varieties. Sweet and tangy, try some of the liqueur on vanilla ice cream or on top of a mango sundae.

COCONUT COQUIMBO

The Coquimbo was a sailing ship that went ashore off the coast of Boynton Beach in January 1909.

It carried a huge cargo of longleaf pine lumber and was destined for Buenos Aires. Though Boynton residents were quick to rescue the crew, the ship itself could not be salvaged.

Within days scores of timber began to wash ashore. Locals scrambled to salvage it, eventually building many of the homes and businesses in the early development of Boynton Beach. To this day the ship's salvaged bell hangs outside of St. Cuthbert's Episcopal Church.

The coconut Coquimbo is a riff on a gimlet.

When we think of sailors and imbibing, we usually think of rum. Pirates as well as low-ranking sailors and crew were given rations of rum. Gin, however, was reserved for officers.

Gin played such a large part of officers' lives that there is a maritime flag called the gin pennant. When hoisted aboard a ship, it is an invitation for other ships officers to come aboard for cocktails.

Ingredients

1 ½ ounce gin
2 ounces coconut water
¾ ounce simple syrup
½ ounce Key lime juice

Directions

Add all ingredients to an ice-filled shaker. Shake vigorously. Strain into a chilled coupe glass. Garnish with a Key lime wheel.

Elevate

Make your Coconut Coquimbo on the beach, with a fresh opened coconut and the fresh coconut water. Skip the coupe glass and the Key lime wheel. Sip from the coconut.

Rich in history...
Rich in Service...
Always exceptional!

PALM BEACH

On January 9, 1878, a Spanish brigantine called The Providencia ran aground the Lake Worth Country. The crew was so intoxicated that they believed they were in Mexico, greeting a few people who met them on the beach with wine, cigars and coconuts. Part of the ship's cargo included 20,000 coconuts.

After weeks of the locals drinking wine and eating coconuts, a local settler purchased the remaining coconuts and tried to sell them for 2 ½ cents each. With only about 1,100 sold, the remainders ended up being planted along the shores of the town that was eventually renamed Palm Beach.

Before long those coconut palms had inundated the area, attracting settlers and inspiring Henry Flagler to build two grand hotels, The Hotel Royal Poinciana and The Palm Beach Inn – known today as The Breakers.

Flagler then plated West Palm Beach as a community for the servants who worked at the hotels while the tracks of his Florida East Coast Railroad crossed Lake Worth so that customers could be delivered directly to his hotels. He later built "Whitehall," his winter home in Palm Beach, which serves as one of America's great historic house museums.

Today's Palm Beach is known for the wealth of its citizens and world-famous shopping on Worth Avenue.

Not as well-known is the fact that not only is Palm Beach County bigger than Rhode Island and Delaware, but 1/3 of Palm Beach County's land mass is taken up by sugar cane fields. One of the largest agricultural counties in the country, Palm Beach produces more sugar cane, corn and bell peppers than any other county in the U.S.

Florida's largest art museum, The Norton, is in West Palm Beach, as is CityPlace and the Antique Row Art and Design District. Edgy galleries and fun shops can be experienced at Northwood Village, and water adventures abound at Shark Wake Park.

Thepalmbeaches.com is an excellent resource for all events in the Palm Beaches. From Boynton's Pirate Fest to candle making classes in Lake Park, there's no shortage of activities here to fit everyone's taste and budget.

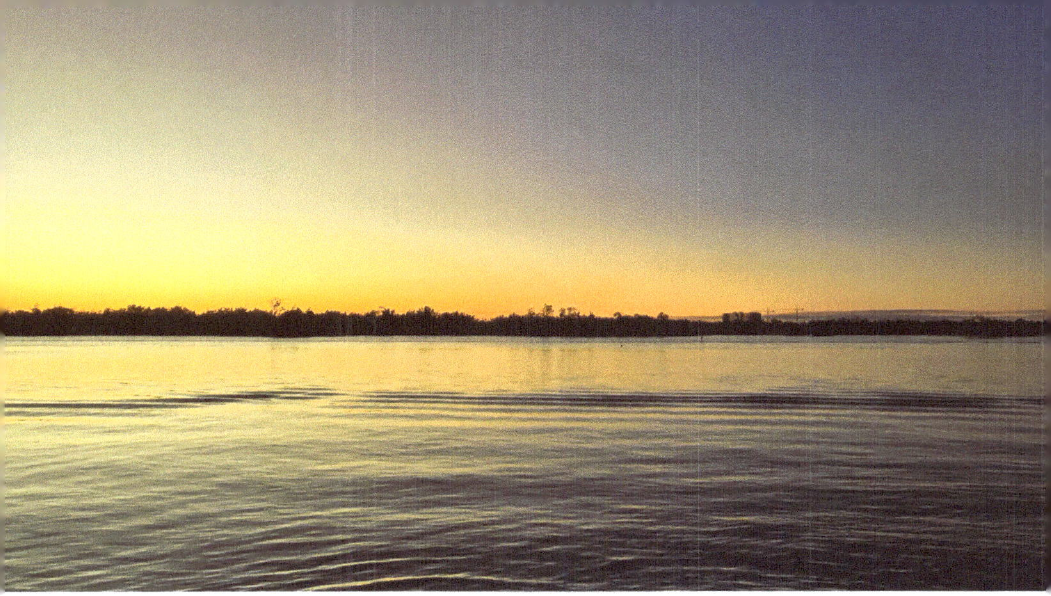

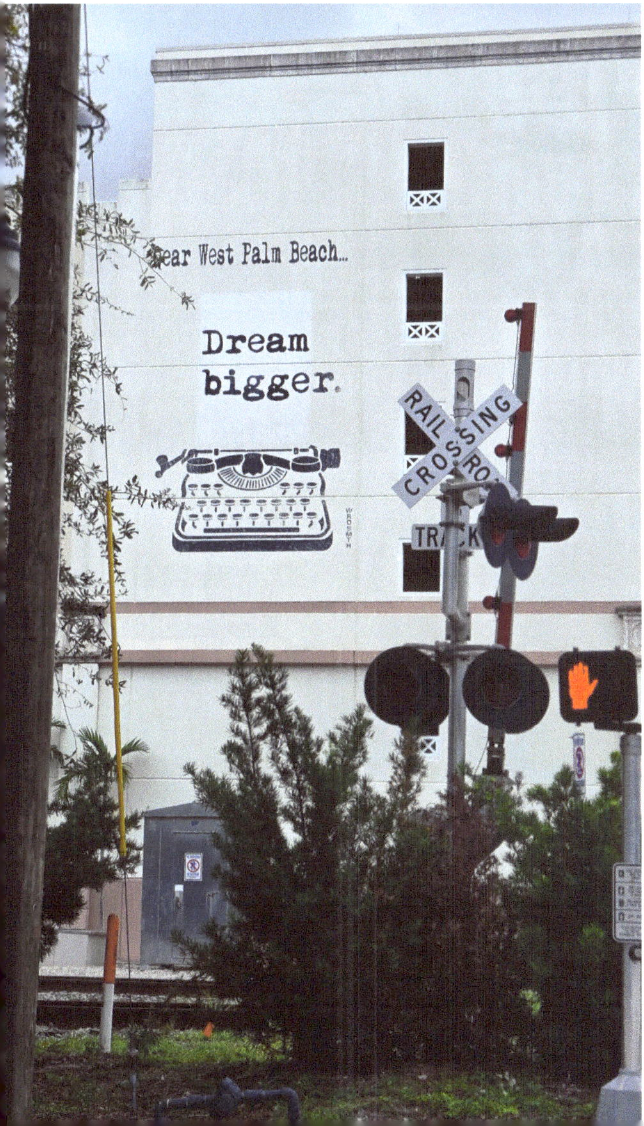
West Palm Beach...
Dream
bigger.
RAIL
CROSSING

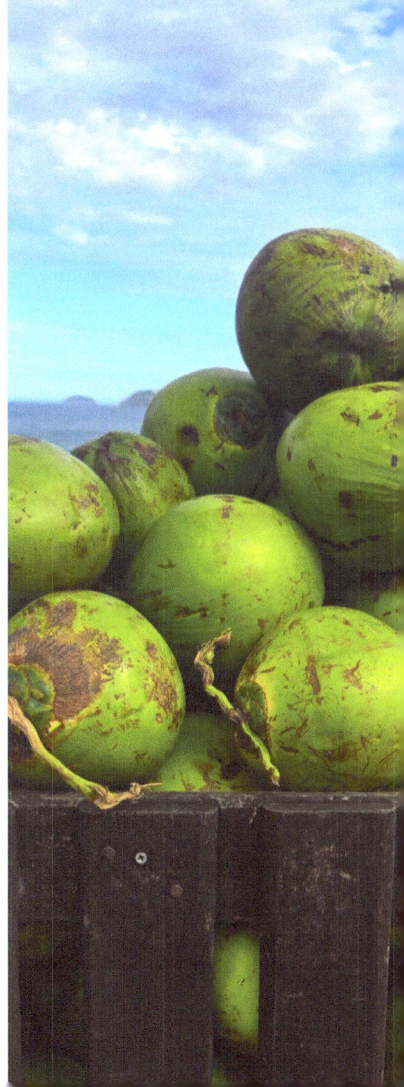

CARAMEL POPCORN OLD FASHIONED

Steel Tie Spirits Co. is a family-owned craft distillery located in a historic building in the warehouse district of West Palm Beach. Distiller Ben Etheridge along with his father Clint have roots in Palm Beach County for almost a century. They celebrate Florida as a source for their inspiration and ingredients.

Such is the case with the Caramel Popcorn Old Fashioned cocktail made with Steel Tie Spirits Co. Spiced Rum. Their flagship spirit, this spiced rum is made with over a dozen pure Florida-grown spices.

Created by mixologist Rob Husted, the cocktail is playfully served on a wooden plank garnished with caramel drizzled popcorn.

Ingredients

1 ounce Steel Tie Black Coral Spiced Rum
1 ounce Black Coral Black Rum
2 ounces caramel peanut popcorn syrup
4 dashes Angostura bitters

Directions

Combine ingredients in a mixing glass with ice. Stir and strain over a large ice cube in a chilled rocks glass. Garnish with a handful of caramel-drizzled popcorn on a wooden board. Place cocktail next to the popcorn.

Caramel Peanut Popcorn Syrup

2 cups Fiddle Faddle caramel popcorn with peanuts
1 cup water

Directions

Combine caramel popcorn with water in a small saucepan. Bring to a boil and immediately lower to a simmer. Cook for 5 minutes. Let cool completely. Strain and refrigerate. Keeps for 5 days.

JIMMY RED SOUR

There is an area in Palm Beach called the Dixie Corridor. Antique row is at the southernmost point, offering a retail haven for lovers of vintage shops, galleries, décor stores and BBQ.

Named "the best locally-owned restaurant in Florida," Tropical Smokehouse is housed in a former Burger King there and helmed by Daniel Boulud trained and James Beard-nominated Chef Rick Mace. Mace makes magic on the bbq, combining traditional techniques with Florida favorites, such as jerk seasoning, yucca, black beans and mojo. Mace also makes a divine cornbread made from Jimmy Red Corn.

A legendary moonshiner's corn, Jimmy Red had dwindled down to just two cobs after the death of the last man known to grow it.

The revival of Jimmy Red is not only good for our planet, it's great for our palates. What better way to enjoy good barbeque than with a good bourbon? This bourbon sour is made with High Wire Distilling Company's Jimmy Red Straight Bourbon Whiskey.

Although we may not think of corn when we think of the Palm Beaches, sweet, local corn is grown in the famous black soil of The Glades Region — a major hub of Florida's agricultural heartland. Here you will find the South Florida Fair and an annual Sweet Corn Fiesta during harvest season.

Ingredients

2 ounces Jimmy Red Straight Bourbon Whiskey
1 ounce lemon juice
1 ounce simple syrup
1 egg white

Directions

Pour all ingredients into a shaker half-filled with ice. Shake until it is very foamy. Strain into a chilled rocks glass. Garnish with a cherry.

Tasting Notes

Jimmy Red Straight Bourbon Whiskey can be identified by its creamy mouthfeel, notes of graham, cinnamon, maple and vanilla.

LUCKY IN LOVE LYCHEETINI

Associated with aphrodisiac powers, the luscious lychee has long been a symbol of love and romance in Chinese culture. You can find fresh lychees in Loxahatchee Groves, an idyllic rural town twenty miles west of downtown West Palm Beach. Make it a day trip by visiting the Loxahatchee National Wildlife Refuge, Lion Country Safari or the Panther Ridge Conservation Center.

Change up the lycheetini by substituting sake for vodka. There is a long connection of Japan and the Palm Beaches, beginning from the establishment of the Yamato Colony in 1904. One of the original farmers, Sukeji Morikami, donated some of his land in Delray Beach. It is now the Morikami Museum and Japanese gardens. The only museum in the U.S. dedicated to Japanese culture, there you will find an extensive Japanese garden, over 7,000 artifacts and special exhibits and events.

Ingredients

1 ½ ounce sake
1 ounce J.F. Hayden's Lychee Liqueur
¼ ounce simple syrup
½ ounce lime juice

Directions

Combine all ingredients in an ice-filled shaker. Shake vigorously. Strain into a chilled martini glass. Garnish with a couple of lychees speared on a cocktail pick.

Tasting Notes

Made with lychees exclusively grown in South Florida, J.F. Hayden's Lychee Liqueur has an exceptional lychee flavor. It is a tart, sweet, floral and fun addition to martinis, margaritas, mojitos and shooters.

LILLY PALOMA

Fill in the blank: Flamingos are to Florida what Lilly _____ is to Palm Beach.

True/False: Both the pink in flamingos and Lilly Pulitzer pink are derived from the beta carotene in shrimp.

Lilly Pulitzer was a socialite from New York who eloped to Palm Beach before it was chic. An enterprising woman, Lilly opened a juice stand utilizing the fruit from her husband's orchards. Sadly, her clothes kept getting stained from juice. She asked her dressmaker to design a dress that would not only hide the stains but fit in such a way that underwear was optional. Don't judge. You'd want to go commando too if you stood in the Florida heat squeezing oranges all day. The customers loved Lilly's dress so much that she started her own clothing line.

Lilly was also known to pour water onto the floor from empty champagne bottles after parties. She would then slide around in the water and do the twist. While many of us know her because of the clothes, Lilly's joie de vie is something we can all remember and celebrate. In her words,

"The Lilly girl is always full of surprises. She lives every day like it's a celebration, never has a dull moment, and makes every hour a happy hour."

Ingredients

2 ounces tequila
1 ounce lime juice
Pinch salt
6 ounces pink Ting soda

Directions

Combine tequila, lime juice and salt in an ice-filled shaker. Shake vigorously and pour into a chilled, ice-filled glass. Top with grapefruit soda. Garnish with a grapefruit slice.

Elevate

Use the Flavourblaster to add a fun, citrus-scented bubble to the top of your drink.

THE LAST TRAIN TO PARADISE

This is a riff on the Last Call cocktail. It was created by Frank Fogarty —bartender at the Detroit Athletic club in 1915 — and was a popular Prohibition-era drink.

Here we substitute Munyon's Paw-Paw liqueur for the green Chartreuse. An herbal liqueur created by Carthusian monks, green Chartreuse is now in short supply. The monks are prioritizing monastic lifestyle over increasing production.

The good news is that a shortage of Chartreuse means that we're encouraged to experiment with other botanical liqueurs to create new cocktails.

The Last Train to Paradise in an homage to both Henry Flagler and Les Standiford. Without Flagler, who knows what the Gold Coast would look like?

Standiford's book, *The Last Train to Paradise*, tells the fascinating story of Flagler's determination to continue his railroad all the way to Key West and the ensuing destruction by hurricane. It is a slice of Florida history that bears repeating.

Ingredients

¾ ounce gin
¾ ounce Munyon's Pawpaw liqueur
¾ ounce maraschino liqueur
¾ ounce freshly squeezed lime juice

Directions

Add all ingredients into an ice-filled shaker. Shake vigorously. Strain into a chilled coupe glass. Garnish with a brandied cherry.

GOLD COAST BAR STOCK

Spirits:

Bourbon

Cachaca

Gin

Pisco

Rum – light and dark

Seco

Scotch

Tequila

Vodka

Liqueurs:

Amaretto

Amara Nonio

Chinola Passion Fruit

Chinola Mango

Chocolate

Cuban Coffee

Curacao

Espresso

Fernet

Lychee

Rum Chata

Syrups, Bitters, Mixers:

Oregat Syrup

Simple Syrup

Flavored Simple Syrups

Angostura Bitters

Lemon Bitters

Peychaud Bitters

Club Soda

Tonic

Flavored Sparkling Waters

Fruit Juices

Garnishes:

Filthy Cherries

Maraschino Cherries

Edible Hibiscus Flowers

Fresh Fruit

Dried Fruit

ACCESSORIES

Show me your bar and I will tell you who you are.

A home bar can be anything from a designated room in the house to a tiki hut in the yard, a rolling bar on the patio or an antique tea cart in the sitting room. It can be a singular cabinet in your kitchen or pantry, or a tray set out on a corner of the counter. Let your space and your personality dictate your choices.

The must-haves of a well-equipped bar are minimal. Complete bar sets can be found on Amazon for little money. The Dollar Tree is an excellent source for odds and ends like pretty paper straws, seasonal glassware, etc. I regularly haunt thrift stores for unique or vintage glassware, shaker tins and measuring glasses.

Basics:		*Upgrade:*
Bar spoon	Hawthorne strainer	Absinthe spoon
Blender	Ice Bucket	Decanter
Bottle opener	Napkins	Pour spouts, bottle
Corkscrew	Measuring cups	Sealers, bottle
Cutting board	Muddler	
Dish towels	Paring knife	
Jigger	Tongs and scoops for ice	
Juice squeezer/ extractor	Shaker	
	Zester	

BEE BROTHER'S
1864

LEMON
BITTERS

For use in Cocktails

5 FL OZ (150 ML)

PERFECT FOR WHISKEY COCKTAILS

Filthy

BLACK CHERRY

WILD ITALIAN AMARENA CHERRIES

NET WT 11 oz (312g)

Wik

Flow

Net Wt 8.8 oz (25

Fun toys:

Clear ice maker

Cocktail smoker with dome

Culinary blowtorch

Flavourblaster

Whipped cream canister for flash infusions (and whipped cream, too)

Accoutrement:

Paper umbrellas

Paper flip-flop stirrers

Peacock feather stirrers

Skewers

Sparklers

Straws

Swizzle sticks

Toothpicks

ACKNOWLEDGEMENTS

They say it takes a village to raise a child. I think it takes an army to create a book. Hours and hours of love, labor and struggle go into the process. If a writer is lucky, as am I, she is surrounded by a dream team of family, friends and a publisher who challenges, nurtures and fosters their creative drive.

Any mistakes or discrepancies in the text are solely my own. As much as I would like to blame my sister Stacey, I cannot. Forgive me for any errors or omissions.

Massive love and thanks to Kit Wohl. I am humbled and awed by your talent, grace and generosity of spirit. You are one of the greatest gifts of my life.

Heartfelt gratitude to Ellen Kanner, Soulful Vegan, friend and writer extraordinaire. You came into my life during a very dark time and have brightened it ever since. You make me laugh out loud more than anyone I know. Your faith in me is a priceless gift that I treasure every day.

Thanks to Casey Bearsch, Leigh Scott and Crystal Murray of LCIX. Your guidance and support mean more than you know. Every writer should be so lucky.

Sam Jweid – artist, creative, photographer. Your abilities know no bounds. Thank you for friendship and your photography.

Joey Schultz became the brother I never had and brought the beautiful Julie Raines into my life. They are constant suppliers of the bar and kitchen gifts I would never think to buy for myself and continuous bearers of joy. Thank you both.

Gabby Aroshas, Chantalle Jweid and Zan Strumfeld are a mini army of ideas, proofreaders, and incredible friends. Thank you.

Gratitude to John Dufresne for years of mentorship, friendship and the gift of your time and wisdom to the writing community.

Thanks to the unparalleled Creative Writing Department at Florida International University and professors Les Standiford, Lynne Barrett, Denise Duhamel, Kimberly Harrison, Campbell McGrath, James Hall and Cindy Chinelly. And I would be remiss if I didn't shout out to administrator Terese Campbell.

Thank you to Debra Hartz Seely, for trusting me to write my first cocktail gig, the Bartender's Best column for the *Sun-Sentinel*.

Thanks to Amy Sherman and the crew at alcoholprofessor.com.

Cheers and thanks to Sam Nelson. Your smiles and lack of complaint while enduring my many mixology experiments is much appreciated. I promise I'll stop leaving mason jars at your house.

South Florida has an abundance of talented and giving professionals who were more than willing to help and guide me on this journey. Special thanks to Larry Carrino and Stephanie Stone of Brustman Carrino PR, Rob Husted and John Kao of Steel Tie Distillery and GiGi Colombo.

South Florida also has an amazing literary community, the Miami Book Fair, and the world's best book store – Books & Books. Mitch Kaplan is nothing short of a hero for all that he and his organization has done for the community.

Thanks also to the friends and family who make up my tasting crew and support system: Abbe Aroshas, Isaac Aroshas, Yakov Aroshas, Ellen Burton, Stephen Bodner, Chrissy Brownlow, Mike Crohn, Michelle Darbro, Richard Dwyer, Fred Ehrenstein, Michael Ehrenstein, Sue Fischer, Dave Fischer, Gordon Garland, Patricia Garland, Rosie Gibson, Becky Hale, Patricia Johnson, Ted Johnson, Izzy Kaplan, Jessie Keefe, David Klein, Melissa Macy, Michelle Ratthe, Michel Repas, Susan Rodriguez, Gail Sherman and Lisa Silverberg.

Appreciation to Dr. Robert Goldman, an incredible humanitarian who has guided and supported my family for more years and in more ways than I can count. Thanks for always being there, Rob.

Thanks to Billy Wohl for the love, acceptance, and gift of your wife's time. We may still sell the trailer and move in with you.

My world would be in a sad state were it not for my Nola family: Stacey Broussard, Sommer Duhon, Christopher Duhon, Eddie Becnel, the kids, the grandkids, the cousins. I miss you all every single day.

I opened this book by dedicating it to you, and I'll close it by thanking you. Laura Powell, Max Silverberg, Sam Silverberg and my son-in-law, Kenton Powell. Chef Remy Powell, Rory Powell and Little Laura Powell. You all are simply the best.

ABOUT THE AUTHOR

Tracey Broussard is a native New Orleanian who has called South Florida home for over 30 years. Editor of the culinary anthology, *Irrepressible Appetites* and the martial arts anthology, *365 Days of the Warrior*, Tracey has written for *The Sun-Sentinel*, *The Miami Herald* and Alcoholprofessor.com.

When she isn't pouring drinks in the sky as a flight attendant for a major airline, she can be found at home creating drinks for her family, friends and on Instagram @tracey.broussard and posting recipes and culinary adventures at her blog www.thebigeasycook.com.

www.ingramcontent.com/pod-product-compliance
Lightning Source LLC
Chambersburg PA
CBHW041730140626
46547CB00024BA/563